Y0-BCO-323

Library of Industrial and Commercial Education and Training

ADVISORY EDITORS:

B. H. Henson, B.Sc.(Econ.) and T. F. West, D.Sc., Ph.D., F.R.I.C., A.M.I.Chem.E.

COMMUNICATIONS
General Editor: M. H. Lovell, C.B.E.

THE LEGAL
LIMITS OF JOURNALISM

THE LEGAL
LIMITS OF JOURNALISM

BY

HERBERT LLOYD

A Solicitor of the Supreme Court
A Fellow of the Institute of Public Relations

PERGAMON PRESS

KD
L5

PERGAMON PRESS LTD.
OXFORD · LONDON · EDINBURGH
NEW YORK · TORONTO · SYDNEY

First Edition 1968   Copyright © 1968 Herbert Lloyd

Library of Congress Catalog Card No. 68-22495.

Printed in Great Britain by Dawson & Goodall Ltd. The Mendip Press, Bath.

08 003866 2

57802

Contents

11. Who Can Sue? (*continued*)

12. Scotland

13. Conclusions

Publisher's Foreword

THE Industrial Training Act has resulted in an increase in the number of people now being trained or re-trained. LICET books are intended to provide suitable texts which will be easy to read and assimilate for those employed in industry and commerce who are receiving further education and training as a part of their employment. It is hoped that they will be particularly suitable for those attending courses leading to the examinations of the City and Guilds of London Institute, the Regional Examining Unions and other examining bodies.

The books are essentially straightforward, simple and practical in their approach and are designed to provide all the basic knowledge required for a particular trade or occupation. They are structured in such a way that the subject is broken down into convenient and progressive components, and are written by authors specially chosen for their expert knowledge and for their practical and teaching experience of their subjects.

Where appropriate, emphasis has been placed on safety training. In some subjects separate manuals on safety and safety training will be provided; in other texts, authors have been encouraged to emphasise safety precautions at relevant points, or to devote a separate chapter to these matters.

LICET books are published in a number of subject divisions, with each division controlled by a specialist editor responsible for selecting authors and providing guidance and advice to both authors and publishers. It is hoped that the series will make an important contribution to further education and industrial training.

ROBERT MAXWELL
Publisher

Foreword

OTHER peoples' affairs are often of compelling and abiding interest to the public. Newspapers, the radio and television are full of reports and pictures which inform—instruct or entertain. It has been said, "All human life is there". But the publication of these accounts of interest, and often drama and glamour, are subject to legal rules. We must always remember that the law touches and affects each of us in almost all aspects of every-day life and that although ninety-five per cent of the work that lawyers undertake has nothing to do with court cases—the remaining five per cent is of special importance to those who communicate—the journalist, reporter, broadcaster, author—to all who provide facts and opinion for publication. For in gathering and passing on his work the journalist must keep constantly in mind the law of defamation and the risk of being sued. Further he must remember that if guilty of contempt of Court he and his employer may be fined or even imprisoned. There are very definite "Legal Limits to Journalism!" I believe this work has succeeded in its aim of setting out simply and readably just what these legal limits are. It gives warning clearly of the dangers that have to be avoided and contains much useful information and good counsel. It should be of real use to all whose job it is to communicate with the public.

The College of Law, HERMON J. B. COCKSHUTT
February 1968

Preface

THIS book has been written specially for those starting a career in journalism—for journalists in the widest sense of the word—those using any form of communication—press, radio, television, photography, or art work, etc. It is intended as a guide to the law of libel and slander—written, spoken, camera, caption, or criticism. It gives an introduction to parliamentary and other privilege, and explains some of the techniques developed by communicators to ensure accuracy wherever possible.

The law on the subject of defamation is complex and extensive and it is hoped that this volume will indicate guide lines, point out pitfalls, and explain the legal limits of journalism.

There are a number of leading works in this field and I would like to acknowledge an indebtedness to the following which I found of particular relevance in preparing this volume.

Current Law, Sweet & Maxwell, Stevens & Sons, 1963.
Modern Advertising Law, by PETER LANGDON-DAVIES, Business Publications London, 1963.
Hatred, Ridicule or Contempt, by JOSEPH DEAN, Constable, 1953.
General Principles of the Law of Torts, by PHILIP S. JAMES, Butterworths, 1964.
Discovering the Law, by JAMES DERRIMAN, University of London Press, 1962.
Halsbury's Laws of England, 3rd edn., vol. 24, Butterworths, 1958.
U.K. Press Gazette, Bouverie Publishing Co. Ltd.
The English and Empire Digest, Butterworths.
The Kemsley Manual of Journalism, Thomson Newspapers.
Essential Law for Journalists, edited by L. C. J. MCNAE, MacGibbon and Kee, 1964.

Above all stands what is, in my opinion, the leading textbook—*Gatley on Libel and Slander*, by R. L. MCEWEN and P. S. C. LEWIS, Sweet & Maxwell.

I am indebted to all authors and publishers for the assistance which I have derived from the above works and for their kind permission to quote from published material in certain cases. All the above works are strongly recommended for further reading.

May I express my gratitude to my old friend Mr. Hermon Cockshutt, of The College of Law, for his wise advice on the treatment of the law stated and for his kindness in writing the Foreword. I am also grateful to Mr. Maurice Lovell for the opportunity to write this book, to Mr. B. G. Tozer for his faith in me; and, finally, I express my appreciation to Mr. Dudley Perkins, Director-General of the Port of London Authority, for his inspiration.

Table of Cases

Adam *v.* Ward, [1917] A.C. 309; 86 L.J.K.B. 849; 117 L.T. 34; 33 T.L.R. 277 H.L.; 32 Digest 129 1608.

Ahmed *v.* Associated Rediffusion (1963), *The Times*, 15 May; Current Law 2014–5.

Arnold *v.* King-Emperor (1914), 83 L.J.P.C. 299; 111 L.T. 324; 30 T.L.R. 462; 24 Cox C.C. 29.

Arthur *v.* Clitherow (1963), *The Times*, 29 June; Current Law 2000.

Att.-Gen. *v.* Mulholland; Att.-Gen. *v.* Foster, [1963] 2 Q.B. 477; 2 W.L.R. 658; 1 All E.R. 767 C.A.; Current Law 2768–9.

Boaks *v.* South London Press (1963), *The Times*, 30 January; Current Law 2005.

Bowen-Rowlands *v.* Argus Press Ltd. (1926), *The Times*, 10 February, 26 March.

Bower *v.* Sunday Pictorial Newspapers Ltd. (1962), *The Times*, 7 July; Current Law 1743.

Boydell *v.* Jones (1838), 4 M. & W. 446; 7 Dowl. 210 1 Horn & H. 408; 51 R.R. 676.

Broadway Approvals *v.* Odhams Press (1965), 1 W.L.R. 805; 109 S.J. 294; 1965 2 All E.R. 523.

Campbell *v.* Spottiswoode (1863), 3 Brs. 769; 32 L.J.Q.B. 185; 8 L.T. 201; 9 Jur. (N.S.) 1069.

Capital and Counties Bank *v.* Henty (1880), 5 C.P.D. 514 C.A.; 7 App. Cas. 741.

Cassidy *v.* Daily Mirror Newspapers Ltd., [1929] All E.R. 117 (C.A.); 2 K.B. 331; 98 L.J.K.B. 595; 141 L.T. 404; 45 T.L.R. 485; 73 Sol. Jo. 348; 32 Digest 67, 898.

Chapman *v.* Lord Ellesmere, [1932] 2 K.B. 431; All E.R. 221; 101 L.J.K.B. 376; 146 L.T. 538; 48 T.L.R. 309; 76 S.J. 248 C.A.; Digest Supp.

Chatterton *v.* Secretary of State for India, [1895] 2 Q.B. 189; 64 L.J.Q.B. 676; 72 L.T. 858; 11 T.L.R. 402; 59 J.P. 596; 14 R. 504 C.A.

B

CHAPTER 1

Introduction

Reputation

What kind of person are you? You may think of yourself as kind, considerate, fairly well-tempered, honest, conscientious, hardworking, and so on. You probably realise that you are in fact many people in one. What do people think of you? Those close to you have their own opinions; mother, brother, sister, schoolteacher, employer, neighbours next door—each have views about you. The sum total of all these opinions is your reputation. You may be known to only a small number of people. A lawyer in a town may be known to most. A film star or leading statesman may have worldwide fame.

Have you ever looked up the word *reputation* in a dictionary? Let us do so now. The *Shorter Oxford Dictionary* tells us that it is a late middle English word which comes from the Latin word *reputationem* which means *computation–consideration*. This is interesting because we are back at the sum total of what people consider. The dictionary goes on to give the modern meaning as "The common or general estimate of a person with respect to character or other qualities; the relative estimation or esteem in which a person is held." The second meaning given is the condition, quality, or fact of being highly regarded or esteemed; also respectability, good report. From the year 1553 it has meant one's good name. Of course, reputation may be bad as well as good. People may be poorly, rather than highly regarded; one's name is not necessarily good. Here is an example of the use of the word given: Addison wrote: "This very old woman had the reputation of a Witch all over the country."

You want people to like you—to think well of you, and you probably behave in such a way that they do. You care about the esteem in which you are rightly held—you are jealous of your reputation. Shakespeare summed the matter up supremely well when he made Othello say:

> Good name in man and woman, dear my lord,
> Is the immediate jewel of their soul.
> Who steals my purse, steals trash; 'tis something, nothing
> 'Twas mine, 'tis his and has been slave to thousands.
> But he that filches from me my good name,
> Robs me of that which not enriches him
> And makes me poor indeed.

How can you be robbed of your good name? How can someone change the favourable opinion people hold about you—wrongly and for the worse? Everyone knows about gossip. The usual picture is of two women chatting by the garden fence or over a cup of tea. You have probably heard someone say, "I know I shouldn't tell you this but . . ." or, "You will never believe me but what do you think she did? . . ."

These gossips are talking about people in a way that affects their reputation. Much of what is spoken—and believe me a very great deal is said every day—is harmless. But sometimes something is said which has far-reaching consequences. Someone's reputation is seriously affected. What if someone told a friend that you were a blackmailer or that you were not fit to hold your job because you were dishonest? You would be very angry and want to do something about it—but what could you do?

You would see a solicitor—tell him the facts and he would advise you whether you had a case against the person who had talked about you. He would be dealing with a branch of the law called defamation.

Defamation—What does it Mean?

To defame is to take away the fair fame of a person, to attack his reputation. Such an attack is usually by the spoken or written word. There are many cases on it—and in 1952 Parliament passed the Defamation Act which consolidated the law dealing with it. We will consider this law later on.

As men and women who are going to communicate with others you must realise how very important it is that you should never at any time say or write anything which will involve you or your employers in a law case brought by someone whose reputation you have attacked. This concerns everyone in journalism, whether you are writing for a newspaper, doing something for radio or T.V., printing, publishing, illustrating, or lecturing. If you communicate in any way you must take great care to observe your legal limits.

You are probably saying to yourself—"I would never say or write anything which was untrue." Quite so—but suppose you got your facts wrong? Someone may be badly hurt by what you have done. You must realise the essential need for the greatest possible accuracy in writing or broadcasting. Much of your work will be dealing with people. People have reputations of which they are proud, and it is your duty as a communicator to respect those worthy of respect.

But what if there is some local villain who deserves to be exposed?—and you regard it as your duty to tell an unsuspecting public what a rogue he is. You may stumble on an exclusive story which you think will make your name as a journalist. You will find the editor to whom you present it very cautious indeed. Not because he does not share your indignation—quite the contrary; and he can probably see even more publicity potential in the story than you can. No. His caution is due to experience, solid experience of the limits of journalism.

You may remember the phrase "Publish and be damned" attributed to the Duke of Wellington. But you cannot rely upon the victim of attacking words being so disdainful as to ignore them. Instead, he may actively resent them. Few can afford to publish such words, particularly at the outset of their careers. Few should in any event do so.

Learning the Law

How then are you to know what you can or cannot do? You may say I'll read the cases on the subject! This would be an immense task. The leading legal textbook about defamation, *Gatley on Libel and Slander*, has nearly 1000 pages, and reports almost 4000 law cases. Most of them are fascinating and we will deal with some later on, but it is not always easy to reconcile many of the decisions which have been handed down by the judges. Try and master the principles. A journalist in the Press or in radio or T.V. may at any time be confronted by a difficult situation and he must have some knowledge of the guide lines which can tell him what he can and cannot do. If a journalist is to perform his work competently and with confidence he must be familiar with some parts of the law. How can you learn? You should seize every chance of getting your senior colleagues to tell you of the pitfalls and, best of all, get to know your legal advisers or a local solicitor. There are certain general principles which lay down the rights and responsibilities of a journalist and we shall look at these before we go on to deal with defamation in detail. I use the expression journalist to cover all who communicate in any way—by the written or spoken word—in print—photography, film, on radio or T.V.—by art work of any kind—printing, publishing, lecturing.

The Freedom of the Press

The Universal Declaration of Human Rights laid down certain essential freedoms that mankind should have of which freedom of expression is one of the most important. This is what it says: "Everyone has the right to freedom of opinion and expression: the right includes freedom to hold opinions without interference and to seek, receive and impart information and ideas through any media and regardless of frontiers". Although this is not precisely the law of the land, it forms the basis upon which many cases have been decided and Acts of Parliament passed. The Press in this country operates in a democracy. There is freedom of speech, freedom to express opinions, freedom to obtain information—

particularly where it is of interest and importance to the public. These freedoms are enjoyed by the journalist and other citizens alike, but there are certain limitations imposed by law. The State must be protected and so must the individual citizen in certain circumstances. If you are doing a story on the army you cannot expect to be allowed to publish the secrets of the nation's master defence plans in case we are attacked. If you are doing a feature on perfumes you cannot expect a manufacturer to welcome your setting out exact details of his secret formula. The law limits what you can say or do. You must not commit treason by betraying information which affects the national security, nor, as we have seen, must you defame innocent people, and, what is more, you must not interfere with legal administration—particularly in the courts of justice—for if you do you may find that you have committed what is called contempt of court. This does not mean that you hold a low opinion of the court or the judge. One of its meanings is doing something which obstructs or prevents a fair trial. You cannot, for example, while a trial is in progress publish a leading article headed "Tom Jones is Guilty". This is a matter for the jury to decide in due course.

The Journalist is a Citizen

A journalist whether of the Press or of radio or T.V., as we have seen, is in the same position as a private citizen. Just because you are a journalist you have no special legal rights to go further than the man in the street can go—you have only the same legal rights to do things, write articles, give talks, take photographs, print or publish and go places, that anyone else has.

You may say at once, "What about press cards?", which reporters carry and which seem to be a wonderful passport to all sorts of places at most interesting times to see exciting events and meet fascinating people. These cards are proof that the holders are members of a recognised professional journalists' organisation, employed as journalists or freelancing. As a result the holders may enjoy privileges but not rights. Many organisations recognise them and give facilities to the press that they would not give to private individuals.

Courts of Law

When you go to a court of law you will usually see a press box conveniently situated so that reporters can hear what the judge, advocates, and witnesses are saying. The existence of the press box, however, does not give the journalist any better rights to be in court than any other member of the public. If the court decides to sit in camera, that is to hear evidence privately (for the word *camera* comes from the Latin word *camara*, meaning a chamber, and *in camera* means in effect in a judge's private room as opposed to open court), a journalist is in the same position as anyone else—unless his presence at those particular proceedings is especially provided for by an Act of Parliament, e.g. proceedings on the winding up of a public company are one of the matters which must be heard in open court.

Privacy

Privacy too is dealt with in the Universal Declaration of Human Rights. Article 12 reads: "No one shall be subjected to arbitrary interference with his privacy, family, home or correspondence, nor to attacks upon his honour and reputation. Everyone has the right to the protection of the law against such interference or attacks."

Recently a Member of Parliament tried to pass a law which would protect the privacy of the individual.

While you are considering the question of where a journalist may go and what he may or may not do you should at the same time have a very clear idea about this subject. Every now and again there is a great outcry about the invasion of privacy, tempers are lost, cameras wrecked, journalists ejected. Has anyone an absolute right to privacy? Probably not. An Englishman's home may be his castle but this by itself does not prohibit anyone calling upon him to ask him a question. So as a journalist you can go anywhere, you can report anything provided you obey the law. You are not limited in any way just because you happen to be a journalist. There are, however, guide lines, and it is the purpose of this book to tell you what some of them are; the pitfalls which exist and how to avoid them. If you are to do your work properly as a journalist you must have a sound knowledge of the legal limits of journalism.

Cases Referred to and the Defamation Act, 1952

A number of reported cases are referred to in this book with the year in which they were decided. In reading them you should bear in mind that the Defamation Act was passed in 1952. This clarified and simplified the law considerably. As a result the cases should be read in the light of the provisions of the Act. This is set out in full at the end of the book and you would do well to read it through carefully.

CHAPTER 2

Defamation

You have already seen that to defame is to take away the fair fame of a person—to attack his reputation. Such attacks are usually made by people talking or writing, but you may be interested to know that defamation can also take many other forms. Even actions or gestures can be defamatory.

Libel and Slander

Defamation is of two kinds—libel and slander. Broadly speaking the law draws the distinction according to the form the defamation takes. If it is permanent it is libel: slander consists of an attack which is transient. Writing, printing, drawings, paintings, photographs, films, television, radio broadcasts, and even a wax effigy have been considered at law to be permanent forms. How can a wax model be a libel? The Chamber of Horrors in Madame Tussauds Waxworks Exhibition is mostly peopled by effigies of notorious murderers and models of the scenes of their crimes. In 1894, between the Chamber itself and the turnstile, was Napoleon Room No. 2 in which, as well as Napoleon and the Duke of Wellington, Mrs. Maybrick an infamous poisoner, and Pigott who was concerned in the Parnell letters case, were also modelled. Here was placed a wax model of Mr. Alfred John Monson, dressed in a brown knickerbocker suit at "the scene of the tragedy" and beside him was a gun labelled "Monson's Gun". He had been tried in Edinburgh on charges of murder and attempted murder and released on a verdict of not proven which is permitted under Scots but not English law. It was held that the verdict did not entitle the Waxworks to make an attack on Mr. Monson's reputation by placing his effigy so close to the entrance to the Chamber of Horrors. Monson won his case but he was awarded only one farthing damages. Spoken words are the most usual form of slander. Significant sounds, looks, signs, or gestures like the hissing of an actor, the deaf and dumb language or an act of gesticulation, such as holding up an empty purse or the like have all at some time or another been held to be capable of being slanderous.

The Right to Sue

You know that you have a right to your good name. The law protects that right. The way it does this is to give another right— to bring an action for damages against your attacker. Not every statement about you which is unfavourable is defamation—the line must be drawn somewhere. It has been drawn by a definition laid down by the supreme legal tribunal in the country—the House of Lords, when Lord Atkin in the case of *Sim* v. *Stretch* which was decided in 1936, said: "Would the words tend to lower Mr. Sim in the estimation of right thinking members of the public generally?" Other cases have decided that if the attack makes people shun you, or avoid you, or exposes you to hatred, ridicule, or contempt, then you have a right of action. You can bring a case against your attacker in the courts. The judge and jury will hear what you have to say, but even if you prove that the words you complain of were written or said, it does not necessarily follow that you will win the case. The writer may have a good defence. What these defences are you will see a little later on.

CHAPTER 3

Libel

To BE a libel, and equally so for slander, the words complained of must tend to lower you in the estimation of right-thinking members of society *generally*. If the words lower you in the estimation only of a particular section of society they are not libellous. You may consider something said about you to be distasteful or objectionable, and your views may be shared only by members of a society to which you belong; you might not win your case, for it is not enough to prove that the words spoken rendered you obnoxious to a limited class of people. It should be proved that the words are such as would produce a bad impression on the minds of average, reasonable men.

Different Forms of Libel

Now let us look at the different forms of libel. The most usual form is by printed or written words—but remember pictures, photographs, cartoons, television pictures, films, can all be libellous. Broadcasting for general reception, although technically the spoken word, is deemed by the Defamation Act, 1952, to fall into the category of libel. Does a libel have to take a certain form? The answer is no. Your attacker may write explicitly, make direct assertion, or insinuate. Cleverness, ingenuity, and skill in indirect writing will not protect your attacker if it is clear you have been libelled.

Innuendo

A libel may contain what is called an innuendo. This word has been a part of the English language since 1564 and it comes from the same word in Latin which means "by nodding at, pointing to, intimating". It was a medieval Latin formula used to introduce a parenthetical explanation "and that is, meaning, to wit, that is to say". In law it is the injurious meaning alleged to be conveyed by words not in themselves (or *per se*) injurious or actionable. Words which, in an action for libel or slander, are usually introduced into the record and issue by the words "meaning thereby", after the expression alleged to have been used. This may not be easy to understand at first reading. To introduce into the record means that it becomes part of the official court record of the case, which includes the pleadings, the written work, the papers prepared to bring the case to trial. Issue here simply means one of the points in dispute to be decided by the judge or, in certain circumstances, the jury. Let us examine it a little more closely. There has to be an injurious meaning. This we know— for libel is an attack which injures your reputation. It is "alleged" —this seems to be a reporter's favourite word. Why? For example, because it does not say a case has been proved or that an offence has been committed or that Mr. Smith *was* at the scene of the crime at the vital moment (Mr. Smith may have a cast-iron alibi). No. The reporter says that it was alleged that Mr. Smith was there when the alleged burglary took place.

Words may be defamatory in their ordinary sense, but the circumstances surrounding their publication may take away the injurious implications. Conversely words which appear to be quite innocent on the face of it may bear another meaning which is clearly an attack on your reputation. Here are some examples. Someone may write of you that you are a trickster. At first sight it would appear in all the circumstances that the words must be defamatory. But what if you are an amateur conjurer who belongs to a social club of like-minded enthusiasts who call themselves The Tricksters? "He is an angel" sounds pretty good and complimentary. But what if "the angels" referred to is the local nickname for a notorious criminal gang? You see now that the real

THE LEGAL LIMITS OF JOURNALISM

significance of words can only be evaluated in the light of all surrounding circumstances. Lord Blackburn in 1882 in trying one of the best-known of libel cases—one in which a firm called Henty & Sons sued the Capital and Counties Bank Ltd., said:

> There are no words so plain that they may not be published with reference to such circumstances, and to such persons knowing these circumstances as to convey a very different meaning from that which would be understood from the same words used under very different circumstances.

What happened in this case was that Henty & Sons sent a circular to customers of the bank saying they would not receive in payment cheques drawn on any of the branches of that bank. There was a run on the bank, whose business was injured.

Was there an innuendo? If so, what do you think it was? The answer is that the circular suggested that the bank was insolvent.

The result of the case may surprise you. It was held that the words complained of were not libellous in themselves and the innuendo suggested, namely that the circular imputed insolvency to them, was *not* the inference which reasonable people would draw. The bank lost the case.

Tolley v. *Fry* (1931)

Another famous case on innuendo concerns a well-known amateur golfer named Tolley. One day he saw an advertisement published by the Fry's chocolate firm. It showed a picture of him playing with a packet of chocolate sticking out of his pocket. Below was written:

> The caddie to Tolley said "Oh Sir,
> Good shot, Sir; that ball see it go, sir;
> My word how it flies
> Like a cartet of Fry's
> They're handy, they're good, and priced low sir."

Mr. Tolley had not been asked and received nothing.

What is the innuendo? The key is in the word amateur: Mr. Tolley was not a professional golfer. It was held that the facts supported the innuendo that Mr. Tolley had prostituted his amateur status for advertising purposes and the advertisement was therefore defamatory to a man in his position.

This is a convenient place to review what we have learnt about innuendo so far.

1. The whole circumstances must be taken into account.
2. There are different kinds of words: those, the ordinary meaning of which makes them defamatory; and those which are not defamatory in the ordinary way and which will only become so if there is an innuendo which can be established.
3. Any words, however defamatory they may appear to be, may be explained away in certain circumstances, and conversely the most innocent of words can become very damaging when all the surrounding circumstances are known.

Here are some examples.

Mrs. Morrison who had been married just a month saw a mistaken announcement in the local newspaper that she had given birth to twins. It was held she had a case.

Mr. Hayes said as a joke that Mr. Donoghue had been caught taking dead bodies out of a churchyard and fined. He was sued and lost. The principle is clear—that a person shall not be allowed to murder another's reputation in jest. But if the words be so spoken that it is obvious to every bystander that only jest is meant, no injury is done. It has been held that even words of praise are actionable if you can prove that they were published ironically.

What do the Words Mean Now?

Times change. Words change their meaning. Look at the various interpretations which have been given to the word *nice* down the centuries. In 1560 it meant foolish, stupid. In 1606 wanton, lascivious. In 1720 tender, delicate, over refined. In 1769 agreeable, delightful. In 1830 kind, considerate, pleasant to others. In 1860 refined, in good taste. The attitude of the public is important. When Elizabeth I reigned you could bring an action if someone called you a witch—for practising witchcraft was then a criminal offence. The place where the libel took place is also of significance—words in one country have a different meaning in another.

Caricatures

What about caricatures? Can a leading politician who is constantly being caricatured sue for defamation? Probably not unless his personal reputation was injured by ridicule. But different considerations apply to ordinary people.

Libellous Words

Many words have been held by the judge to be capable of bearing a libellous meaning. Here are some of them: rogue, rascal, dishonest, crook, swindler, coward, liar, immoral, racketeer, intolerant, oppressive.

Insolvency and Credit

There are certain words which have a special significance. For example, it is libellous to write and publish that a man is bankrupt or insolvent or that he is unable to pay his just debts if in fact none of these things is true; but it is not libellous to write that you owe money. For this does not necessarily imply that you cannot or will not pay what you owe. While we are on the subject of money, this seems a convenient moment to examine the position of banks and cheques.

Banks and Cheques

These have given rise to a number of cases dealing with defamation. A bank is very much like a person and stays in business as long as the public has confidence in it. Accordingly, a false accusation that affects its credit—injuring it by causing mistrust—may be libellous. A bank, too, can libel. So far as cheques are concerned it can be defamatory to write that your cheque has been dishonoured—the inference being that you are dishonest or insolvent, or at least are guilty of bad faith. But be careful about "R/D", the notorious "Refer to drawer" which is sometimes written on a cheque by a bank. Mr. Justice Scrutton in a delightful passage said: "I doubt whether the words 'Refer to drawer' written on a cheque returned to the payee is libellous. In my opinion in their ordinary meaning they amount to a statement by the bank 'We are not paying. Go back to the drawer and ask him why,' " But even this is now in doubt by a November 1967 decision.

Other Libels

Statements dealing with decrees and judgments of the courts need to be handled with special care.

Strangely enough it is not libellous to write of a man that he has had a judgment taken against him.

Care must be taken, too, when dealing with reports concerning a man's business, particularly when reports deal with the credit of a firm or its relationships with employees past or present.

The law makes special provisions for allegations of insanity, or that the person attacked suffers from a contagious or repulsive disease. You may think that insanity excites pity not ridicule, and consequently an allegation that a person is of unsound mind does not necessarily expose him to hatred, ridicule, or contempt, but the practical effect of such an allegation usually is to cause the sufferer to be shunned, and the same thing applies to certain diseases.

What happens if you are compared with Ananias or Judas?

15

c

You can be libelled if your character is compared with those of infamous persons. Mr. Justice Erle said as far back as 1848:

> Nothing is easier than to bring persons into contempt by allusion to names well known in history or by mention of animals to which certain ideas are attached. The Court will take judicial notice that such words as Judas have an application very generally known indeed, which application is likely to bring into contempt a person against whom it is directed.

Photographs

You can be libelled by a photograph. One of the most interesting cases on this point was where an advertisement headed "Leg Appeal" showed one girl's head and shoulders and below the bare legs of another lady. The inference was that the owner of the head did not have suitable limbs of her own to complete the picture. She was a model. She sued and she won. [*Griffiths* v. *Bondor* (1935).]

Speeches

Be on your guard when reporting after-dinner speeches. The speaker may make humorous remarks which may also be defamatory. In a case on this it was held that the man attacked had the right to say that it was beside the point that he did not care what the speaker said about him after dinner. He did not choose to be made an object of ridicule, good natured or otherwise, in a newspaper merely to amuse a number of people who knew nothing of him. [*Dolby* v. *Newnes* (1887).]

Immorality—Chastity—Illegitimacy

You may not feel that chastity is as important as it was. Nothing could be more wrong as you will find to your cost if you impute unchastity to those who appear to have led blameless lives. The stigma of illegitimacy has mercifully begun to pass away, but this again presents a danger area to the innocent journalist. It can be libellous to write that a man is illegitimate, and his mother, too, may have a cause of action, for you have imputed unchastity to her.

Death

What if someone writes that you are dead, when you are very much alive? No libel—unless your reputation is affected.

Libels on a Man in his Work

The law has for a long time given special protection to the reputation of people in their office, profession, calling, trade, or business. Its provisions have been codified in the Defamation Act, 1952. We shall deal with this more fully in due course but in the meantime you should note that any written or printed words which disparage a man in the way of his office, profession, or trade may constitute a libel. Not everything which is detrimental is actionable. If someone writes that you have ceased to carry on your business you may be very angry and inconvenienced, and, indeed, your business may suffer injury, but it is not necessarily a libel. Why? Because the bare statement lacks the essential ingredient in that it neither denigrates the way in which you carry on your business nor points to the lack of a necessary factor for its successful running. If the words complained of do not involve any reflection upon your personal character or the manner in which you carry out your official or professional duties or trade, they are not actionable *per se*.

Especial care must be taken in dealing with dismissals from employment and the reasons why.

Office-holders—The Professions

There is a type of case dealing with office-holders which arises when an attack is made alleging corruption, dishonesty, or fraud, or that the office-holder is incapable of carrying out his duties.

It is also actionable to impute unfitness for a profession or office because of lack of the necessary ability. The leading cases on this type of defamation deal with the Church, the law, and doctors. If you write of a clergyman that he has been guilty of immorality or drunkenness you do so at your peril. The Rev. Kelly won a case in 1869 against Mr. Sherlock who wrote that the clergyman had desecrated part of his church by turning it into a cooking department. The Rev. Curtis succeeded against Mr. Argus in 1915, in a New York case, when the complaint was that he had juggled with the collections.

Naturally you would expect lawyers to have the law relating to themselves explicit. It is. Mr. Boydell won his case for defamation against Mr. Jones in 1838, the allegation being that he had been guilty of sharp practice in his profession.

Other matters which have been the subject of court decisions include writing that a lawyer had given his client's case away; that he had been struck off the rolls; or suspended from practice.

What about doctors? To call one a quack may be libellous, for Lord Alverston defined a quack as one who exploits the timid and the credulous for his own advantage. And, of course, to say that the doctor caused the death of the patient by careless treatment may also be actionable, as also are allegations of unprofessional conduct.

As a possible budding journalist, the cases dealing with literary men will probably have a special appeal to you. If you are wrongly accused of a plagiarism, or represented as a literary freak or a writer or publisher of obscene articles, you can probably sue and win.

It has been held libellous to say of an architect of a public building that his appointment can be regarded in no other light than a public calamity.

Sport and entertainment, too, has its share of libel cases—jockeys riding unfairly, vulgar actresses, horizontal boxers, incompetent football coaches, have all featured as allegations in libel cases.

Note that libels on professions must refer to lawful professions.

Trade

We have seen that one of the most important things a trader has is his credit. If this is impeached an action may lie. This can be done by imputing bankruptcy or insolvency. If you are accused of using false weights or selling worthless goods, or that you employ sweated labour, you may have a case. Mr. Justice Chitty summed it up in 1892 when he said:

> If Mr. Marshall states of Mr. Collard who is a trader earning his liveli-hood by dealing in articles of trade, anything, be what it may, the natural consequences of uttering which would be to injure the trade of Mr. Collard, then Mr. Collard can bring an action. The allegation was that Mr. Collard employed sweated labour—and this was calculated to bring him and his business into hatred and contempt, and to deter respectable persons from dealing with him.

Allegations of incompetence and want of judgment may be libellous. A distinction should, however, be drawn between persons and goods. If your goods alone are attacked and not your personal or trading character, there is no ground for an action for libel. But there is a catch here. Goods can be *slandered*, usually by a malicious falsehood.

Malicious Falsehood—Slander of Title and of Goods

But have you any remedy if your *goods* are attacked? Section 3 of the Defamation Act provides that in an action for slander of goods, slander of title or other malicious falsehood, you need no longer prove special damage if the attack is calculated to cause you pecuniary damage and is in permanent form, or if the attack is calculated to cause pecuniary damage in respect of your office, profession, calling, trade, or business carried on by you at the time of publication.

Consider the following case.

In 1892 Mr. Evans published in his newspaper that a firm of boilermakers and engineers, Ratcliffe & Sons, had ceased to exist. As a result the firm lost a good deal of business and sued. The jury found that the statement was not a libel but that it was an untrue statement not published in good faith and awarded £120 damages.

What do you have to prove to succeed in an action for malicious falsehood?

1. That what was said referred to your goods.
2. The words were untrue.
3. They were published maliciously—and maliciously here means with a dishonest or improper motive.
4. Unless covered by section 3 of the Defamation Act, you suffered special damage.

But remember—mere "puffing"—i.e. commending your own goods, is not actionable.

In 1910 the Advertisers Protection Society published a monthly circular in which they said: "*Observer*. We are informed that it is now selling about 5,000." The circulation was actually 30,000. The paper sued for libel alleging that the statement was false and that they had suffered damage. Mr. Justice Darling said that he did not think that a mere statement that the circulation of a news-paper was 5,000 could amount to libel and held that so far as the action was based on libel there was no case. Dealing with dis-paraging the plaintiff's property he said they would succeed if the jury agreed that actual damage had been caused by an untrue statement *maliciously made*. The jury found there was no damage and *The Observer* lost the case.

Another point to watch here is "knocking copy". Everyone wants the world to think his product is better than the others—and goes to great lengths in advertising to convince the public this is so. You can only sue if someone imputes some specific defect to your product. If you are associated with consumer protection societies or trade journals this is a branch of the law to which you must give the closest attention.

Supposing someone wrote of the paper you are working for that it has a column for the advertisements of quack doctors, or that it was the lowest now in circulation and this fact was sub-mitted to the consideration of advertisers, then it might be fair to assume that the statements disparaging your paper involves an imputation upon the personal character of your newspaper pro-prietors and editors.

Proof

What do you have to prove to win?

1. Words are false;
2. they were published maliciously;
3. that the words are defamatory of you in your personal or business or trading character; that they are not merely a disparagement of your goods; and that
4. the words are reasonably capable of bearing the meaning complained of—and it is for a jury to decide what the meaning really is.

We have so far examined the different types of defamation. You can see that there are many kinds and that you can be libelled in all sorts of ways. The examples given should warn you of what can happen and put you on your guard. Above all it should drive home the absolute necessity for scrupulous accuracy in all you do, say, or write and the need for care and caution.

It is not always easy to see the distinction between defaming a person and disparaging his goods. A libel on a thing may be a libel on a person. If you write Lloyd's beer is adulterated, that would be a libel upon him in his trade, not because of the allegation that the beer was bad but because the language would import deceit and malpractice on the part of the brewer. In cases like this the onus is on you to prove that the words are defamatory of you in your personal or business or trading character and not merely an attack on your goods.

These, then, are some of the different forms that libel cases can take. You will probably not find it easy to see a consistent pattern running through the various decisions of the judges. Do not worry. The courts have found themselves in the same difficulty. In *Broadway Approvals* v. *Odhams Press* (1965), in the Court of Appeal Lord Justice Russell said: "To the comparative newcomer, the law of libel seems to have characteristics of such complication and subtlety that I wonder whether a jury on retirement can readily distinguish their heads from their heels" (*Gatley on Libel and Slander*, Preface to 6th edn., 1967). I have set out a large number of examples in this section in order that you may see how easy it is to become involved in libel proceedings and the great need for care both in checking all the available facts and in the actual writing of copy.

CHAPTER 4

Slander

Proof

Although most of your work as journalists may be of a permanent nature and therefore governed by the rules relating to libel, you should also know the essentials of the other type of defamation —slander. Slander is defamation by the spoken word or in some other transitory form. There are four types of case you can bring if you are slandered *without having to prove that you have suffered special damage as a result*. They are:

1. That you have been accused of a crime punishable by imprisonment, e.g. if you are called a thief or a blackmailer. The crime need not be indictable, that is, of the most serious kind, and it is not necessary that the exact offence be specified. The words must impute a criminal offence but slang words are sufficient. The intention of the person attacking you is immaterial and as in the case of libel the whole of the surrounding circumstances have to be considered. If, however, something is said of you which is really vulgar abuse, particularly if it is said in the heat of passion, e.g. that you are a blackguard or a rascal, you are unlikely to win your case.

2. The second category includes words imputing a contagious disease. Leprosy, venereal diseases, the plague, scarlet fever are included. Insanity is not—because it is not catching— and the imputation must be that the individual has the disease now and not merely that he once had it.

3. Words which are calculated to disparage a man in any office he holds, or his profession, calling, trade, or business. The rules here are much the same as for libel. Imputing insolvency to traders, misconduct to clergymen, dishonesty to lawyers, are examples.
4. The fourth class of case where you can sue without proving special damage is if you are a woman or girl and someone imputes unchastity to you. Direct terms are not essential to be a slander. It is enough if the words used would be understood by ordinary people to convey a specific imputation of unchastity. An allegation that a woman is a lesbian has been held to be an imputation of unchastity.

Special Damage

When spoken words complained of do not come under any one of the four types given above, you can only win your case if you can prove that you have suffered special damage. This means the loss of some material advantage which is capable of being estimated in money, such as being sacked from your job or losing a client or customer, or even the loss of free entertainment or the hospitality of your friends. A judge once said bodily illness is not the natural or the ordinary consequence of speaking slanderous words, and consequence of mental suffering does not constitute special damage enabling you to bring an action for slander. Incidentally, the damage you suffer must have been suffered before you bring your action. Haddan was thrown out of Lott's public house by a servant who said he was drunk. Haddan told his father, who threatened to remove his son from the board of a family company unless he could clear his name. Haddan sued Lott for slander and pleaded as special damage the threat of his ceasing to be a board member. He lost. He had not actually suffered the damage.

The special damage must be the natural, reasonable, and direct result of the defendant's words.

A gossip once told a father that his daughter had had a child by her master. The father went to see the master and asked him if it were true. He replied that it was quite false, but sacked the girl from a job as governess to his children because he felt that it might damage both their characters if she remained. The courts held that the gossip should pay; the special damage was proved. Another case concerned a gossip who told a man that his wife was all but seduced by the doctor before her marriage. The man thereupon turned his wife out of the house. The judge held that the man's conduct was not natural or reasonable so could not constitute special damage.

The jury are the people who have to decide what damage has been proved and whether it was a result of what the defendant said. The judge decides whether the damage constitutes special damage and, if so, whether it was the natural and probable result of the words complained of.

CHAPTER 5

Publication

You cannot win your case for defamation unless you prove that the words you complain about were published. But what does publication mean? Simply—communication. The law is dealing not just with what was said or written, but passing it on to someone else. Quite a number of people can get involved in this. For example, in the case of a defamatory book the author, publisher, printer, may all be joined in the proceedings. You do not have to tell the public generally. One other person is sufficient. If someone writes you and tells you falsely that Mr. A. is a liar, this is publication. Telegrams and postcards can also constitute publication.

But you must remember that a man's reputation is not the good opinion he has of himself, but the estimation in which others hold him. Accordingly, if someone writes to you privately defaming you, this is not publication. Publication can happen by any act which passes on the defamatory meaning. If you read a defamatory letter out loud to a third party, that is publication. If you hand a defamatory letter to a typist to be copied, that is publication. Likewise if you use a dictating machine and get it transcribed.

But not all communications which affect your reputation, even if publication of the libel takes place, are actionable. Sometimes what is called privilege applies, for there are certain occasions when, in the public interest, freedom of speech must take precedence over the private rights of an individual so far as his reputation is concerned. We will deal with this in detail a little later on.

There can be intentional and unintentional publication.

Letters

So far as letters are concerned, if you write to a particular person you will not be responsible except for publication to that person. Where publication is not intentional, the jury must decide whether the effect of sending a letter is likely to be that someone other than the plaintiff will open it. If you had been a member of the jury in the following 1962 case, what would your verdict have been? Mrs. Theaker and Mrs. Richardson quarrelled. Mrs. Richardson wrote a letter to Mrs. Theaker falsely accusing her amongst other things of being a prostitute and brothel keeper. She typed the name and address on a cheap manilla envelope, sealed the back with Sellotape, and put it in Mrs. Theaker's letterbox. *Mr.* Theaker picked it up off the mat, opened it, and read it. He said he thought it looked like an election address and there was nothing to suggest it was confidential. Well? How would you have decided the case? Libel, or no libel? Publication? The Court held on the facts that taking into account the appearance of the unstamped envelope it was proper to infer that someone other than Mrs. Theaker would open it. She won her case and Mrs. Richardson was liable. If the person to whom you wrote passes the letter on to someone else, that is his own action for which you cannot be held responsible. Some interesting cases have arisen where letters have been sent to addresses where the writer knew they were likely to be opened by clerks; in these cases it has usually been held to be publication. The words must pass on the defamatory meaning for the passing to be publication. If, for example, you write in a foreign language that third parties do not understand there is no publication. But what if you never meant to publish the libel? You may still be held liable unless you can show that there was no want of care on your part. Cases sometimes arise where people raise their voices, not realising they are being overheard. If they should have realised, they can be held liable for the shouted slander. What would you say of the following case of unintentional publication?

Unintentional Publication

In 1875 a Mr. Whitaker, who was the printer of a journal, made a mistake in setting out *London Gazette* announcements. Instead of putting an entry about a Mr. Shepheard under the heading "Dissolution of Partnerships" he put it under "First Meetings in Bankruptcy". There was no malice, and a full apology was published as soon as the mistake was discovered. Nevertheless, Mr. Shepheard won his case and recovered £50 damages.

But you may not win if the libel was unintentional and there is no want of care. What do you have to prove? Not directly that the words were actually communicated. In certain circumstances this may be inferred. For example, if someone libels you on a postcard which is posted, the court will take judicial notice of the document, that it is a postcard, and will presume in the absence of evidence to the contrary that it will be read by people other than the person to whom it is addressed.

Who is Liable?

Who is liable for publication? If the libel is contained in a book, or a periodical, or a newspaper, everyone who took part in publishing it, or procuring its publication, is, on the face of it, liable. This can include the editor, the printer, the journalist, the newsagent, the publisher.

The law, by the way, does in fact protect people who are not printers or authors and who have only taken a subordinate part, the most common examples being those who sell newspapers. A newsvendor will not be liable if he did not know the book or paper contained the libel, or that the book or paper was of such a kind that it was likely to contain a libel, and he was not negligent in not knowing. The newsagent would have to prove these things to escape liability. With a newspaper a good deal depends on its reputation. The law realises that there must be a commonsense approach to the problem of what the newsvendor can reasonably be expected to know. As far back as 1885 this was laid down in a case when Mr. Emmens sued Mr. Pottle for publishing a libel. Mr. Pottle was a newsvendor who sold a newspaper containing a libel. The jury came to the conclusion that Mr. Pottle did not know that the newspaper contained a libel, that he was not negligent in not knowing, and that Mr. Pottle did not know or ought not to have known that the newspaper concerned was of such a kind that it was likely to print libels. The Court of Appeal held that Mr. Pottle was an innocent disseminator and so Mr. Emmens lost his case.

More than one person can be involved in publishing a libel. The B.B.C. could be held liable as joint publishers of a libel on radio or television. In a newspaper, the newsvendor, proprietor, publisher, editor, and printer may all be jointly and severally responsible. If you have been libelled you can sue one or all the people you claim have defamed you.

The law, too, recognises the special relationship of husband and wife. In law for many purposes they are regarded as one person. So if you tell your husband or your wife something defamatory about someone else you cannot be sued. But this does not stop you suing if someone says something defamatory to you about your spouse.

What about publication outside this country? Generally speaking, you can bring an action based on publication abroad if the law of that country recognises it as a wrongful act. The act complained of must be wrongful both by the law of this country and by the law of the country where it was committed. Remember, too, that publications you send abroad should be lawful in the countries to which they are sent.

Identity—Innocent Libel—Reference to the Plaintiff

If you are going to succeed in your action for defamation you must prove several things. Firstly, that the defendant was responsible for publishing the words you complain of; next that those words are defamatory—that is, they tend to lower your reputation in the opinion of right-thinking people; and, most important, that you identify yourself as the person libelled.

Does your name actually have to appear in the statement complained of? No. The test in every case is—would the words be understood by reasonable people to refer to you? The defendant can use blanks, asterisks, initials, or fancy names or descriptions. It does not matter so long as they are such as reasonably in the circumstance would lead people acquainted with you to believe that you were the person referred to. It is not necessary for the reader to know all the facts. You must be understood to be the person defamed. If someone writes that all news broadcasters were dishonest no particular news broadcaster could sue unless there was something to identify the particular individual.

The intention to refer to you is immaterial. It does not matter whether the libeller did not intend to refer to you or did not even know of your existence. Section 4 of the Defamation Act, 1952, has a special provision dealing with this which we shall consider later on.

This is one of the most serious of all legal points concerning journalists. What if you did not know that a man you name even exists—in other words, so that you could not conceivably have intended to refer to him? The law was laid down very clearly in the case of *Hulton* v. *Jones* (1909), when the question was put: "Would the words complained of be understood by reasonable people who knew the plaintiff to refer to him? If so, they are published of and concerning the plaintiff no matter what the intention of the defendant may have been." This case is so important that we shall deal with it in some detail. A very readable account is given in *Hatred, Ridicule or Contempt*—a book of libel cases by Joseph Dean published by Constable, 1953. The following is a précis.

Hulton v. *Jones* and Other Cases

Artemus Jones was at one time a sub-editor of the *Sunday Chronicle* and subsequently joined the *Daily Telegraph*, writing chiefly from the Press Gallery. In 1901 he was called to the Bar.

In 1908 the *Sunday Chronicle* published a feature article headed "Motor Mad Dieppe" by a Mr. Dawbarn.

> Upon the terrace marches the world, attracted by the motor races—a world immensely pleased with itself and minded to draw a wealth of inspiration, and incidentally of golden cocktails, from any scheme to speed the passing hour. Whist! There is Artemus Jones with a woman who is not his wife, who must be, you know—the other thing! whispers a fair neighbour of mine excitedly into her bosom friend's ear. Really is it not surprising how certain of our fellow countrymen behave when they come abroad. Who would suppose by his goings on that he was a churchwarden at Peckham? No one, indeed, would assume that Jones in the atmosphere of London would take on so austere a job as the duties of churchwarden. Here in the atmosphere of Dieppe, on the French side of the Channel, he is the life and soul of the gay little band that haunts the casino and turns night into day, beside betraying a most unholy delight in the society of female butterflies.

Artemus Jones was in court at Chester Assizes when he read the article, as did his colleagues. There was comment. Subsequently, wherever he went on the circuit he met the same reaction. He instructed his solicitor to ask for an apology and damages. The *Sunday Chronicle* denied that the article referred to him—said they would put in a disclaim, which they did without first of all showing it to Artemus Jones or his solicitor. This is what the disclaim said:

> It seems hardly necessary for us to state that the imaginary Mr. Artemus Jones referred to in our article was not Mr. Thomas Artemus Jones, barrister, but, as he has complained to us, we gladly publish this paragraph in order to remove any possible misunderstanding and to satisfy Mr. Thomas Artemus Jones we had no intention whatsoever of referring to him.

Mr. Artemus Jones was not satisfied and sued E. Hulton & Co., the printers, proprietors, and publishers of the *Sunday Chronicle*. The trial took place at Manchester Assizes. Artemus Jones gave evidence himself and five witnesses testified that they knew him or knew of him and believed he was the person mentioned in the article. The judge said that if readers of ordinary intelligence understood the article as referring to Artemus Jones, it did not matter if there was one or fifty of them. The editor of the *Sunday Chronicle* and the author of the article swore they had never

31

D

heard of Artemus Jones. The Peckham churchwarden was an imaginary character. In his summing up the judge said that if people chose to publish articles of this kind, they did so at their own risk. The writer's actual intentions were irrelevant. Would the ordinary reader think that the Peckham churchwarden was imaginary or a real person called Artemus Jones? He won his case and was awarded £1750 damages.

Hulton appealed and the fundamental nature of a libel was fully explored. There were two main points of view. Firstly, that a libel was the publication of a malicious untruth by one man about another, and for this the law provided a remedy. But could you defame someone who you believe exists only in your imagination? For you are not writing about someone you know, and how can you have malice for someone you do not know exists?

Secondly, every man is presumed at law to intend the natural consequences of his acts. If you write in such a way that the natural consequence is to lead people to believe you were referring to someone they knew, it does not matter if you have never ever heard of him. He has suffered from an attack by your writing, why should you not pay? Malice was not essential. Hulton went to the Court of Appeal and to the House of Lords. Both courts rejected the appeal. Artemus Jones got his damages and so it was laid down that it was immaterial that the defendant did not know of the plaintiff. The test was—would reasonable people believe the words referred to the man they knew?

The consequences of the case were far-reaching. Lord Chief Justice Goddard said it added a terror to authorship. You will probably have noticed at the beginning of a film or a book an announcement that all the characters are fictitious and that any resemblance to any living person is coincidental. Writers and publishers became very much alive to the dangers of the situation and the disclaim notice was one of the first results of the *Jones* v. *Hulton* case.

The effects on Fleet Street were severe. Year after year cases were brought against newspapers for libelling persons they never knew existed and therefore could not have intended to refer to. A typical example took place in 1928. The *Cassidy Case* cost the

Daily Mirror £500 damages and costs for publishing in a gossip column the photographs of a man and a woman and underneath the words: "Mr. M. Corrigan, the racehorse owner, and Miss X whose engagement has been announced." This was correct. The press photographer had been asked by Corrigan to take the photographs when they were at Hurst Park racecourse. He gave the girl's name and address and permission for the engagement to be reported. Corrigan's real name was Cassidy. He was a married man. The real Mrs. Cassidy sued the *Daily Mirror.*

What do you think was the libel she complained of? The innuendo meant in her view that she was dissolute, an immoral woman, who had imposed on her friends and acquaintances by pretending to be a respectable married woman when in fact she was living in open adultery with her husband. They had separated, but he still came to see her occasionally. She won.

Another case occurred in 1939 when Harold Newstead, a barber from Camberwell, sued the *London Express Newspaper* because they published an article about the trial of Harold Newstead, a Camberwell man, for bigamy.

> Why do people commit Bigamy?
> Harold Newstead, 30 year old Camberwell man, who was jailed for nine months, liked having two wives at once. Married legally for the second time in 1932, his legal wife is pictured above right, he unlawfully married nineteen year old . . . (left above). He said "I kept them both until the police interfered".

The account of the trial was correct, but the fantastic thing here is that the report concerned another Harold Newstead, a barman from Camberwell. Newstead won his case although he only got nominal damages. Sir Wilfred Greene, then Master of the Rolls, said: "If there is a risk of coincidence it ought, I think, to be borne not by the innocent party to whom the words were held to refer but by the party who puts them in circulation."

The rules then laid down were harsh, but their effects have to some extent been mitigated by the Defamation Act, 1952, which is set out in full at the end of this book. Section 4 of the Act deals specifically with unintentional libel and the ways in which amends can be made. These will be dealt with later.

33

57802

Libel on a Group

Often articles are written about a group of people. If someone wrote all journalists are dishonest no particular writer could sue him unless there was something to point to that particular individual. But have a care. This does not give you the freedom to write what you will about a body of people. If the group is capable of being clearly defined they may be able to sue. Examples are all the directors of a particular company, or the clergy attached to a particular church, or all members of a particular club. And remember that each and every member can issue a writ for defamation against you. In an 1895 case in Scotland a Mr. Macleod said that members of a presbytery should not have taken part in proceedings against their minister for intemperance because of their own excesses. It was held that each member of the presbytery could sue. (*Macphail* v. *Macleod* (1895)).

A young journalist may write an article with the heading "Either Jones or Smith is guilty"—and go on to reveal some scandal. If the attack is libellous he cannot put up the defence that he did not say which one was guilty. If you wrongly attack all members of a jury in a case, all can sue.

Repetition and Republication

The general principle is that if someone knowingly publishes a libel about you he will be held responsible—whether the libel originated with him or not. It will be no defence for him to plead that he got the libel from someone else and, indeed, said so at the time. The fact that one person publishes a libel about you does not entitle someone else to do the same thing. Mr. Justice Best summed it up when he said: "Wrong is not to be justified or even excused by wrong." Here is an example. In 1854 Mr. Ainslie published a pamphlet in which he reprinted extracts from a letter written by someone else libelling Mr. Tidman. Mr. Ainslie honestly believed the statements in the letter to be true, but it was held he had no defence to an action for republication. Journalists must be very careful about this. The fact that a libel has been published in another newspaper is no defence if you republish it. The only thing that indicating the source of the article will do to help you is that it may mitigate any damages awarded against you. The same rules apply to slander.

What if, at the time you repeat the libel, you say you doubt whether it is true? Here you may think you have a good defence. But you would be wrong. It will make no difference to your liability. No one's reputation would be safe if just by saying you did not believe a rumour made you immune from proceedings by the person you defame.

What happens if you libel someone in an article and it is then republished? Are you liable for the repetition? The answer is no. You are not responsible for unauthorised republications for they are not the reasonable consequence of your original publication. Of course, you would be liable if you authorised the repetition, or where republication was a natural result of what you did or where the person to whom you published the original libel was under some special duty to pass the statement on.

A young reporter was told by a man a startling story attacking a prominent local man's reputation, saying it would make good copy for the paper. The story was printed and the man was held liable for he had authorised the republication. The same position arises where a contributor writes an article which turns out to be defamatory. The author is liable for the damage caused by publication. This has been settled law for a long time. As far back as 1890 it was held that Mr. Moiguard, who printed a libel in one edition of his paper, was liable for republication in other editions in other countries, for he knew quite well that the libel would be repeated, and the man libelled—Mr. Whitney—won his case.

Are there any defences to this kind of claim? Yes. If they can prove they were innocent disseminators, i.e. they can prove that they did not know and could not reasonably be expected to know what they were circulating was defamatory, they will have a good defence. It has been said that a person who buys a book is not bound to read it at his peril before he lends it to a friend.

CHAPTER 6

What do the Words Mean?—Prove it!

THE words complained of must be given their ordinary meaning—which is the meaning in which reasonable men of ordinary intelligence with the ordinary man's general knowledge and experience of worldly affairs would be likely to understand them. This was laid down by Chief Justice Lord Mansfield as long ago as 1777.

We have already seen in the case brought by the Capital and Counties Bank against Mr. Henty that where the words are said to have an innuendo or secondary meaning, the manner, occasion, persons concerned, and all the circumstances affecting their meaning in the particular case must be considered. If someone complains that what you have written has another meaning which is defamatory it is up to him to prove it. What you yourself intended to mean is immaterial in deciding whether the words are libellous, and the words must be construed as a whole, in context. For example, if you accuse someone of libelling you in a newspaper, you are entitled to have taken into account not only the offending words but the paragraph, the whole article, and the heading.

When a case comes to court the first question to be decided is whether the words are capable of a defamatory meaning. This is a matter for the judge. Whether the words complained of are defamatory or not is a question of fact for the jury.

Liberace v. *Daily Mirror*

A case dealing with the construction of words was that brought by Liberace against the *Daily Mirror* in 1959. The *Mirror* published an article in which Liberace was described as "The Summit of Sex—the pinnacle of masculine, feminine and neuter. Everything that He, She, or It can ever want". And, "This deadly, winking, sniggering, snuggling, chromium-plated, scent-impregnated, luminous, quivering, giggling, fruit-flavoured, mincing, ice-covered heap of mother love". The Court was not asked to consider any innuendo as to the meaning of the words complained of. Mr. Justice Salmon asked the jury to decide whether the words (with the exception of fruit-flavoured) connoted homosexuality. The jury said they did and Liberace won. The judge, however, in his judgment said that he had come to the conclusion that the words were just capable of the meaning the jury had found, although he was by no means certain he would have come to the same conclusion of fact.

In *Lewis* v. *Daily Telegraph* (1964), Lord Reid said: "Here there would be nothing libellous in saying that an inquiry into the company's affairs was proceeding: the inquiry might be by a statistician or other expert. The sting is in inferences drawn from the fact that it is the fraud squad which is making the inquiry."

Intended Meaning Immaterial

The intended meaning is immaterial. The question is, not what the writer intended, but what reasonable readers thought was intended. Liability for libel does not depend on the intention of the defamer but on the fact of the defamation. If someone attacks you in ordinary defamatory language, all you have to prove is publication.

If the words complained of on the face of it do not appear to be defamatory, an innuendo or secondary meaning must be pleaded, and in court you must prove not only publication but also that there were facts known to the persons to whom the words or matter were published which might reasonably lead them to understand the words in the attacking way alleged in the innuendo or secondary or hidden meaning. Here is an example of innuendo.

Frank Hough was a popular boxer. The *Daily Express* published an article about him which read: "Frank Hough's curly-headed wife sees every fight. 'I should be more in suspense at home', she says. 'I always get nervous when he gets in the ring, although I know he won't get hurt. Nothing puts him off his food. He always gets a cooked meal at night, however late it is when he gets in.' " The curly-headed lady was not Mr. Hough's wife and the real Mrs. Hough sued. She produced two witnesses. They said they knew Mrs. Hough was the real wife of Frank because they had been at the wedding. There was no suggestion that they had been misled by the article into thinking Mrs. Hough had been living and bearing children in sin. They were very angry about the other so-called Mrs. Hough. In 1940 the Court of Appeal held that it was true that in the eyes of these two witnesses the article cast no imputation on their friend, but others might read it differently. It was no more essential for anyone to have understood the libel for what it was than it was necessary for anyone to have believed in it. The jury awarded Mrs. Hough 50 guineas damages.

Cases on Meanings

Let us now consider a few more cases where the court had to consider whether the words complained of were defamatory.

In 1962 the *Sunday Pictorial* published a report in which they said that a Mr. Bower had been convicted of attempted murder and sentenced to life imprisonment. The paper falsely published that he had been sent to Parkhurst and had had a complete mental breakdown. The jury found that the words complained of were defamatory in their natural meaning and that the statement that he had been sent to Parkhurst was defamatory in the sense that the words meant that he had earlier convictions. Damages of £6500 were awarded for the first libel and £750 for the second. (*The Times*, 7 July; *Current Law* 1743.)

In *Wait* v. *Associated Newspapers Ltd.* the plaintiffs, directors of a football club which was losing money and to which they had all donated generously, put forward a plan for summer football. The defendants, in their newspaper, commented on the plan as being selfish and sounded "a note of caution to the foolish men who want to change our habits to try to grab a bit more money".

In the plaintiff's libel action they claimed that the words meant that they were interested in football primarily for the money and were urging their plan for purely selfish and mercenary reasons. Mr. Justice Paull, on the verdict of a jury, held that there should be a judgment for each of the plaintiffs for £250. (*The Times*, 18 May 1963; *Current Law* 1999.)

Here is a case where the alleged defamatory meaning could only be understood by experts. The defendant, the B.B.C., was the publisher and author of an article which erroneously ascribed to the plaintiff, Mr. Mollo, an expert on contract bridge, the advocacy of a bid at bridge which was said to be insupportable. In the plaintiff's libel action, no innuendo was pleaded. McNair J. dismissing the action, held that the words would not be regarded by ordinary people as disparaging the plaintiff's character, although they might damage his reputation in the minds of those with special knowledge of modern bridge practice. (*The Times*, 2 February 1963; *Current Law* 2003.)

In 1963 Clitherow, the national organiser for the League against Cruel Sports, alleged to representatives of the national press that Arthur had thrashed his horse at Badminton trials with criminal severity. His comments were printed. Clitherow, with certain reservations, admitted publication and apologised to Arthur who was awarded £7500 damages and costs. (*The Times*, 29 June 1963; *Current Law* 2000.)

Television Broadcast

Associated Rediffusion made a television broadcast relating to prostitution in Stepney which included a picture of Mr. Ahmed's club and cafe. Ahmed sued for libel. The jury held that the broadcast did not mean that Ahmed was knowingly providing facilities for indulgence in prostitution, but that the premises were in fact frequented by persons seeking and providing indulgence in prostitution and that neither meaning was defamatory to Ahmed and both were in any event true. The T.V. company won. (*The Times*, 15 May 1963; *Current Law* 2014.)

39

CHAPTER 7

Defences

You have already seen something of the various types of actions for defamation which can be brought. Now we will consider in some depth the defences which can be pleaded. It is most important that you understand these clearly, for paradoxically, if you know the defences you will probably be a better journalist whether of the Press, radio, or T.V. and do your work in such a way that you will keep out of trouble. Knowledge of the defences are some of the main keys to safe and effective writing.

Seventeen Possible Defences in Actions of Defamation

The following is probably the best and most comprehensive list of defences that are possible in actions of defamation. It is based on *Halsbury's Laws of England*, 3rd edn., vol. 24, p. 10.

1. You never published any of the words complained of.
2. The words complained of did not refer to the plaintiff.
3. The words complained of did not bear any defamatory meaning.
4. The words complained of were true in substance and in fact. (Justification.)
5. The words complained of were published on an occasion of absolute privilege. (Absolute privilege.)

6. The words complained of were published *bona fide* (in good faith) and without malice towards the plaintiff on an occasion of qualified privilege. (Qualified privilege.)
7. The words complained of were fair and *bona fide* comment without malice towards the plaintiff on facts truly stated which were a matter of public interest. (Fair comment.)
8. Offer of amends has been made with a defence of unintentional defamation.
9. In the case of libel in a newspaper or other periodical publication, apology and payment into court.
10. The publication of the words complained of was with the consent and by the authority of the plaintiff.
11. Accord and satisfaction. (Agreement to forego claim.)
12. Written release from liability.
13. Lapse of time—the Statute of Limitation.
14. *Res judicata* (the matter has already been dealt with by the court).
15. The publication was made abroad and is justifiable in the country of publication.
16. In actions of slander (i) the words complained of were mere words of heat or vulgar abuse; (ii) that the words complained of were not actionable without proof of special damage and that no special damage is alleged, or that the special damage alleged is too remote in law; (iii) the words complained of were not calculated to disparage the plaintiff in any office, profession, calling, trade, or business held or carried on by him at any material time.
17. Death of the party concerned.

If you are unfortunate enough to have a libel claim made against you, it is essential that all the facts be most carefully examined to see whether any of the defences set out above are available to you.

We shall now deal with some of the more important ones in detail. They are: justification; fair comment; absolute privilege; and qualified privilege.

Justification

This means that the statement was true in substance and in fact. This can be a risky defence because if you lose you have aggravated the matter. It does not succeed very often. Every relevant fact has to be strictly proved and this is not an easy thing to do when some time has elapsed since publication; hence the necessity of making and keeping for a reasonable time careful notes. Saying a woman is a thief and has stolen £20 cannot be justified by proving that she stole a hen. Nor is stealing a watch the same thing as stealing a clock. The whole slander has to be answered.

If you write of a man that you believe he has committed murder you cannot justify publication by proving that you did believe it. You can only justify it by proving the fact of the murder. In 1940 the English and Scottish Co-operative Properties Mortgage and Investment Society prepared their annual accounts. Their auditor advised them to include an item on the profit side. The official auditor did not agree. In order to resolve the dispute and with no intention of imputing any improper motives to the Society, the Registrar of Friendly Societies issued a summons for wrongly making a false "Return of Profits". Odhams Press reported the matter under the heading "False Profit Return Charge against Society" and subsequently pleaded justification as a defence to libel proceedings. The Court of Appeal held that the word "false" was ambiguous and might mean fraudulent or it might mean incorrect. The jury had come to the right decision and the defence failed. Owing to the difficulties which so often arose in pleading the defence successfully, the matter is specially dealt with by section 5 of the Defamation Act, 1952.

This laid down that if you are sued for a libel in respect of words containing two or more distinct charges against the person you attacked, your defence of justification shall not fail by reason only that you cannot prove the truth of every charge you made. But there is a proviso. What you can not prove must not materially injure the plaintiff's reputation having regard to the remaining charges you made against him. If you write an article which contains statements of fact and of opinion, you must be prepared to prove the facts true and the statements correct. The Commercial

Publishing Company in 1907 published a statement that a Mr. Smith had been arrested on a criminal charge and added a headline and comments which said in effect that the charge was true. They pleaded justification, but the court held it was not enough to prove the arrest on the published charges—the comment which imputed that the charge was true or assumed the guilt of Mr. Smith had to be justified as well. A journalist's reputation is often in the hands of the sub-editor. Headlines are of vital importance and the heading is just as material and important as the text. For an editor to write a heading "How Doctor Smith treats his patients" when the paragraph refers to one case only, even if the case itself was accurately reported—the headline implying that Dr. Smith generally treated his patients badly, cannot be justified.

Substantial justification is sufficient. You do not have to prove the truth of every word of the libel—only as much as meets the sting of the charge. Slight inaccuracies of detail will not prevent the success of the defence, for example in writing that a man had been sentenced to a fine of £1 with the alternative of three weeks imprisonment, whereas in fact the alternative was fourteen days. A material inaccuracy means the defence will fail. If you write that Mr. Weaver has committed various acts of cruelty by beating a horse, including knocking out an eye, proof of all the acts of cruelty except knocking out the eye will not be sufficient. Why? Because your statement that he knocked the horse's eye out imputes a much greater degree of cruelty than the accusation of beating. Here are two more cases dealing with justification.

A man serving a sentence of preventive detention claimed damages for an article in the *People* which, he alleged, meant that he had committed a murder for which he had been tried and acquitted in 1944. The article had been written by prosecuting counsel in the case. The jury found that it had the meaning contended but that it was true. The *People* won the case. [*Loughams v. Odhams Press* (1963). *The Times*, 14 February; *Current Law* 2007.]

In a case decided in 1963, £3500 damages were awarded to a man who was a vice-president of a football supporters' club for an attack which alleged that he had been "posing as an official of the club or of the supporters club" and to have been causing some nuisance by seeking admission to matches on this pretext. A plea of justification failed. (*Vaughan* v. *Palmer* (1963); *Current Law* 2008.)

Fair Comment

Fair comment is a very important defence and probably the one most often pleaded in the courts. It is a defence to an action for libel that the words complained of are fair comment on a matter of public interest. This has both scope and limitations, and the implications should be clearly understood. Let us first examine the difference between justification and fair comment. In justification you rely on the truth of what you have written, thus negativing a claim made by the person you have attacked to a reputation he does not deserve. In fair comment you rely upon the honesty of your statement of opinion. It may not matter whether in an objective sense what you have written is true or not but the facts must be true for the comment to be fair. *Remember that fair comment can only be used as a defence where the matter which is commented on is a matter of public interest.*

> A newspaper has the right, and no greater or higher right to make comment upon a public officer or person occupying a public situation than an ordinary citizen would have; [and again] To whatever lengths the subject in general may go, so also may the journalist, but apart from statute law, his privilege is no other and no higher. The range of his assertions, his criticisms, or his comments, is as wide as, and no wider than, that of every other subject. No privilege attaches to his position.

So said Lord Shaw in the case of *Arnold* v. *King-Emperor* (1914). Lord Justice Scott wrote in 1943: "The right of fair comment is one of the fundamental rights of free speech and writing which are so dear to the British nation, and it is of vital importance to the rule of law on which we depend for our personal freedom." (*Lyon* v. *Daily Telegraph* (1943), which is reported more fully later on.)

44

Fact and Comment

Let us now have a look at the meaning of fair comment and the meaning of public interest. A comment is a statement of opinion on facts. If you write that what John Smith has done is disgraceful, that is a comment. If you write that John Smith did a disgraceful act you are maybe stating a fact, not giving an opinion. It is one thing to comment upon or criticise, even with severity, the acknowledged or proved acts of a public man, and quite another to assert that he has been guilty of particular acts of misconduct. If you make statements of fact and are sued it is up to you to prove the facts to be true.

The same rules apply to the criticism of music, books, plays, films, and television programmes. If an author writes a play or a book, or a composer a musical work, he is submitting that work to the public and so inviting comment. Any words written must be read in their context and any allegation must be recognisable as comment not fact. A comment cannot be fair if it is distorted by malice. In 1906 a malicious reviewer wrote a criticism of a biography by a Mr. Thomas. He headed the paragraph, "Mangled Remains" and cast aspersions on Mr. Thomas's literary ability. He also made allegations of fact which were untrue. It was found that he had personal spite against Mr. Thomas. The Court of Appeal held that it was proper to take malice into account and since the jury had found the review was distorted by malice the defendant could not rely upon fair comment. [*Thomas* v. *Bradbury Agnew & Co.* (1904-7).]

Another important case decided that the defence of fair comment may succeed where the facts which form the basis of the comment are not stated by the commentator provided that the nature of the facts can be reasonably inferred from the comment itself. This is the case of *Kemsley* v. *Foot* (1952). What happened?

Mr. Foot published an attack headed "Lower than Kemsley" on a newspaper with which Lord Kemsley was not connected. He sued for libel alleging as innuendo that the effect of Mr. Foot's statement was that the newspapers he owned were of a low character. The defence was fair comment. The Court decided that having regard to all the circumstances, the matter under comment could reasonably be inferred from the heading. It was a newspaper that was attacked and as it was a matter of common knowledge that Lord Kemsley also owned newspapers, it was sufficiently clear that the standard of those newspapers was under attack.

In 1862 Mr. Pickburn published in his newspaper a report of a medical officer of health which asserted that Mr. Popham, a local chemist and druggist, had been issuing false medical certificates and suggested that he should be prosecuted for forgery. It was decided that the report could not be held to be fair comment. Do you agree? If so why?

It was argued that this comment might be justified as being in the public interest. But this is not a comment—it is a statement of fact. *Moral*—never mix up your comments with the facts upon which they are based. One useful tip is always to set out your facts first. Only after you have done this should you go on to comment. The whole should be printed in such a way that the reader can easily see what is fact and what is comment or criticism and so be in a much better position to judge the value of the latter.

There is no complete definition of fair comment. You will probably have realised very quickly that each case has to be considered individually and it is not easy to draw from the many actions which have been fought the fundamental principles which are an essential part of the law if it is to have any certainty.

However, there are three conditions which should be fulfilled. Learn these and you will have your own do it yourself test kit. They are (1) that subject to section 6 of the Defamation Act, 1952, the comment was based on facts set out truthfully; (2) there must be no suggestion that the creator of the work criticised had dishonourable or corrupt motives, unless of course such imputations were warranted by the facts; and, finally, (3) it must be the honest expression of the writer's real opinion.

The Defamation Act, 1952, section 6, provides that if you are sued for libel over something which you have published consisting partly of fact and partly of opinion, your defence of fair comment need not fail simply because you do not prove the truth of every allegation you have made, provided that your expression of opinion is fair comment on what you do prove. Fair comment is a defence to comment only. You will not succeed with your defence unless you prove that the facts upon which the comment was made are *substantially* true. It is a question of relative importance. You must not invent facts or take lies from others and comment upon them as though they were true. One of the leading cases on this was decided in 1886 when a newspaper editor (Shepstone) published serious allegations about Davis, the Resident Commissioner of Zululand. It said that not only had he himself violently assaulted a Zulu chief, but had ordered his native police officers to attack others. Assuming these statements to be true they strongly commented upon his conduct. The stories were quite untrue. He was awarded £500 damages.

Newspaper Comments

What about newspaper comments? You can comment on the evidence given at a trial and the conduct of a magistrate in dismissing a charge without hearing the whole of the evidence. But you must be fair and give all the relevant facts. In S. Africa in 1926 White Ltd. published that Harris was convicted at assizes of a felony and commented adversely on the fact—but did not go on to say that the conviction was quashed on appeal. Harris won. The defence of fair comment by White failed.

There are certain exceptions to this rule; that the defence of fair comment will fail unless the facts are truly stated, the chief of which are where comment is made on facts stated in a privileged document such as a parliamentary paper or judicial proceedings. We shall deal with privilege in the next chapter.

If you impute corrupt or dishonourable motives you will make your comment unfair unless you can prove that the imputation is warranted by the facts. Spottiswoode attacked Campbell by saying in an article that Campbell was trying to increase the sales of a newspaper he owned by a false pretence that he was seeking to propagate the gospel among the Chinese. It was held in 1863 that this was outside the limits of fair comment. Criticism can cease to be criticism and become a defamatory libel. The true test is now laid down by section 6 of the Act of 1952.

E

Lyon v. Daily Telegraph

So far as honest comment is concerned lack of motive is essential. Exaggerated comment is not necessarily unfair. The statement must be within the domains of criticism. Consider the case of *Lyon* v. *Daily Telegraph* (1943). The Lyons were radio entertainers. The *Daily Telegraph* published a letter which read:

Flabby Amusement

To the Editor of the Daily Telegraph

SIR,

Early Sunday evening at Church time there was put on the air a costly broadcast which is an insult to British intelligence. The type of humour consists of a vulgar exchange of abuse. One comedian alludes to the other as a "louse" and his chief humorous contribution is to say at intervals, "I'm laughing me blooming 'ead off". The woman artist has a fair voice and sometimes sings a good song, but for the most part she indulges in vulgar wisecracks. We must be a nation of lunatics to permit such a waste of money for such a sordid show.

Yours sincerely,

A. WINSLOW

The Vicarage, Wallington Road, Winchester.

The address was fictitious and there appeared to be no such person as A. Winslow—such was no evidence of malice and the letter itself did not exceed the bounds of fair comment. It was on a matter of public interest. Accordingly the defence of fair comment could be pleaded by the *Daily Telegraph.*

The case raised an interesting point on the duties of editors and correspondents. Lord Justice Scott said that he could not accept that there was a general rule of law making it the duty of every newspaper to verify the signature and address of a writer before publishing a letter. On public grounds it would be desirable to do so, but to hold that the absence of such verification destroys the plea of fair comment would put too great a burden on newspapers. He went on to say that it would be a burden so deterrent in practice as would reduce the valuable contribution to public discussion of correspondence in the Press. If the comment were fair and the editor published it solely in the public interest, he could not see any hardship to the person criticised if the paper succeeded in the plea of fair comment.

He concluded with a forthright defence of the press in the following words:

> To impose such a burden—namely that the onus should be on the newspaper of proving that the writer of the letter honestly held the views expressed—is not desirable from the public point of view and is contrary to the existing law of fair comment. The more freedom in art criticism, music, literature, painting and drama, the better for the aesthetic welfare of the public.

You can see how difficult it is to define fair comment. Everyone has his own standards. We all have our own ideas of good taste and fair play and so in the end it always comes back to the ordinary man. Lord Esher when Master of the Rolls in 1887 summed it up in this way: "Would any fair man, however prejudiced he may be, however exaggerated or obstinate his views, have said what this criticism has said." (*Merivale* v. *Carson* (1887).)

Justice Bray said:

> When you come to a question of fair comment you ought to be extremely liberal, and in a matter of this kind—a matter relating to the administration of the licensing laws—you ought to be extremely liberal, because it is a matter on which men's minds are moved, in which people who do know entertain very, very strong opinions, and if they use strong language every allowance should be made in their favour . . .

Putting it in a nutshell he said: "Could a fair-minded man, holding a strong view, holding perhaps an obstinate view, holding perhaps a prejudiced view—could a fair-minded man have been capable of writing this?" Which you will observe is totally different from the question, "Do you agree with what he has said?"

Public Interest

Now let us turn to public interest. What are matters of public interest? They are many—dealing with anything which may fairly be said to invite comment or challenge public attention. Examples are the prospectus for a new company, advertisements, the conduct of hoteliers, people at public meetings, newspapers. Public figures on stage and screen ask for criticism and get it. If you go on the stage to exhibit yourself to the public or give or organise any kind of performance to which the public is invited, you may be freely criticised—remember the 1967 altercation between the Royal Court Theatre and Milton Shulman. You cannot sue over such criticism, however severe or incorrect it may be so long as it is the honest expression of the critic's real views and not mere abuse or invective under the guise of criticism. Any place to which the public have the right of access may be commented on. Books, films, television programmes, broadcasting, pictures, music, photographs, sculpture, architecture—all works of art—if placed before the public invite fair comment on a matter of public interest. Note—the private life of an author, artist, or journalist, is not necessarily a matter of public interest. But in this type of case there are certain conditions which must be complied with if the defence of fair comment is to succeed. They were laid down in the case of *McQuire* v. *Western Morning News* in 1903. Robert L. McEwen and P. S. C. Lewis, in the sixth edition of *Gatley on Libel and Slander*, the leading textbook on the subject, summarised them as follows:

> However severe, even in a sense unjust, the criticism may be, the critic will not be liable, provided
>
> (1) he does not misrepresent the contents of the book;
> (2) he does not go out of his way to attack the character of the author;
> (3) his criticisms may be fairly termed criticism; and
> (4) his criticism is the honest expression of his real opinion.
>
> The principle underlying the plea of fair comment is that a man who appeals to the public must be content to be judged by the public.

Local authorities and their administration are a fruitful source of topic for criticism as, indeed, is the management of public institutions—such as hospitals, prisons, railways, and the like.

The Administration of Justice

What about the law? The due administration of justice is undoubtedly a matter of public interest and therefore fair matter for public comment. But you must be very careful to wait until a trial is over before commenting upon it. Then the evidence, the conduct of trial, and verdict may be lawfully commented on. There are grave difficulties about commenting pending or during a trial, as it could prejudice a fair trial and result in your being accused of contempt of court.

Contempt of Court

The leading case on this was the one where the editor of the *Daily Mirror* was sent to prison for three months in 1949 while the paper was fined £10,000. The contempt arose over the "acid bath murder" when Haigh was accused of murdering a woman and dissolving her body in acid. While he was remanded in custody the *Daily Mirror* printed a comment which said that so far five murders had been attributed to him and the names of those concerned were given. The case came before the very forthright Lord Chief Justice Goddard who in the course of his judgment on 25 March 1949 pronounced:

> Not only does it describe him as a vampire but in addition to saying he has been charged with a particular murder of which he has been charged, these articles go on to say not merely that he is charged with other murders, but that he has committed others, and gives the names of persons whom they say he has murdered and a photograph of a person whom he is said to have murdered and described the way in which she was murdered.

He went on to say that was a scandalous and wicked case. The fact that Haigh subsequently confessed to nine acid-bath murders did not prevent the *Mirror* from being in contempt of court.

Other Matters of Public Interest

Other matters of public interest are church affairs, sermons— (it was comment on a sermon which was the first step leading to the abdication of Edward VIII), politics, state matters, the proceedings of the House of Commons, royal commissions, government reports, and the public conduct of any man who holds or seeks a public office or position of public trust. It is the judge who decides whether the matter commented on is one of public interest and whether there is any evidence of unfairness, and the jury whether it was fair comment.

Cases on Fair Comment

Here are some more cases on fair comment.

In the case of *Plummer* v. *Charman* (1962)—"To say of a man supporting a bill to make incitement to race hatred unlawful that he had come down on the side of 'coloured spivs and their vice dens' was held defamatory, not a statement of fact, nor fair comment." (*The Times*, 25 October; *Current Law* 1756.)

"Commander Boaks of Streatham whom I usually regard as nutty, sends me a plan for Tower Bridge that I, for once, think brilliant." Defamatory or not? What do you think? A jury decided they were not in the case of *Boaks* v. *South London Press* (1963). (*The Times*, 30 January; *Current Law* 2005.)

In *Saleh* v. *Odhams Press* (1963), Mr. Saleh, a Muslim carrying on business and living in England, complained of an article headed, "Girl Bride Cost Him £800" which appeared in an Odhams newspaper, alleging that it meant he treated his wife as a chattel. Odhams denied this meaning and pleaded justification and fair comment. In the course of the trial the reporter admitted that she did not recognise the published article as her "story". The editor did not give evidence, Saleh was awarded £750 damages. (*Current Law* 2006.)

In *Showerings* v. *Postgate* (1965), the defendant published an article referring to wines which could be obtained in public houses and said: "Beware particularly of a thing called Babycham which looks like champagne. If you read the label carefully you will find it is made of pears. But wines they mostly are, and tricks cannot stop the change." The plaintiffs, the manufacturers of Babycham, claimed damages for libel. The defendant pleaded fair comment and the reply alleged malice. Held on a verdict of the jury there should be judgment for the defendant. (*Current Law* 2259.)

CHAPTER 8

Absolute Privilege

SOMETIMES public interest makes it reasonable for the right to freedom of speech to overcome the right to private reputation. When this happens the law treats the circumstances as "privileged". There are two kinds of privilege—"absolute" and "qualified". Absolute privilege means that no action for defamation can be brought in respect of any statement however untrue, false, or wantonly and maliciously made. Qualified privilege can be rebutted by proof of malice in the sense of using the privilege for a purpose for which it was not intended or by proof of excessive publication. We will deal first with the more important matters covered by absolute privilege. No action lies for defamatory statements, however false or maliciously made:

(1) in the course of debates or proceedings in Parliament;

(2) in the course of state communications;

(3) in the course of judicial proceedings and proceedings before tribunals exercising functions similar to those of a court of justice;

(4) in reports published by order of either House of Parliament;

(5) in fair, accurate, and contemporaneous reports in a newspaper or by broadcasting of public proceedings before a court exercising judicial authority within the United Kingdom.

Parliamentary Proceedings

You cannot sue a member of either House of Parliament for defamatory words spoken in the course of any Parliamentary debate or proceeding. Note that the protection here only applies to words spoken *in the House*. If the M.P. causes his speech to be printed in a newspaper he will be liable in the ordinary way. Absolute privilege extends to statements contained in petitions addressed to Parliament and to evidence given before select committees.

State Communications

You cannot sue an army, navy, or air force officer for libelling you in any report he makes to his superior officer. Neither can you sue any officer of State for any defamatory statement he puts into an official report made by him to the head of his department. Why do you think this rule was made? In a famous case brought by Chatterton against the Secretary of State for India in 1895 it was said by the Master of the Rolls, Lord Esher, that the reason was that it would be injurious to the public interest that such an inquiry should be allowed because it would tend to take from an officer of State, his freedom of action in matters concerning the public. If he could be sued, malice could be alleged against him and his independence prejudiced. It is desirable that public servants should be able to write freely on matters affecting the public service without fear of an action. The Civil Service of this country has a very high reputation. In case you are wondering who are the officers of State, look them up in *Whitaker's Almanack*. Some of them are ministers of the Crown, senior officers of the armed forces, and high commissioners. The Lord Great Chamberlain is the sixth officer of State. The documents complained of cannot be produced in evidence, nor can any witness say what they contain, for the obvious reason that they may reveal state secrets. This gives rise to a certain amount of criticism at times. Journalists can be suspicious if, when following a good lead, they find that the head of a department of Government states that the production of a particular document by the department would be injurious to the public interest. The decision may be made by the man who may have the most to cover up and conceal. Absolute privilege is given to official publications such as the *London Gazette*.

Judicial Proceedings

Statements made in judicial proceedings may be privileged. When the Royal Aquarium and Summer and Winter Garden Society Ltd. sued Parkinson in 1892, Lord Justice Lopes said:

> No action of libel or slander lies, whether against judges, counsel, witnesses or parties for words written or spoken in the course of any proceeding before any court recognised by law, and this though the words written or spoken were written or spoken maliciously without any justification or excuse, and from personal ill will and anger against the person defamed. It is immaterial whether the proceedings take place in open court or in private, for if such actions were allowed persons performing their duty would be constantly in fear of actions.

This rule is founded on public policy and should be studied very carefully indeed. The protection incidentally is given not only to what is said at a trial but also to statements such as those made by solicitors preparing the necessary documents to bring the case to court. A judge is not privileged to be malicious but he is privileged from inquiry as to whether he is malicious. The High Court, county courts, quarter sessions, coroners' courts, magistrates' courts, courts martial, are all covered. A witness is protected by a rule established for the benefit of the public—if he were not he would only have to say: "I shall not give you any information at all." Advocates are privileged in what they do and say before the courts; the law allows them that privilege because it is for the advantage of the administration of justice that they should possess an unlimited freedom of speech. Here is an example of the rule applied to a court case.

In 1883 a man was charged before the magistrates with administering drugs to the inmates of Munster's house in order to facilitate the commission of a burglary at it. Munster was the prosecutor

55

and Lamb was the defending solicitor. There was some evidence, although of a very slight character, that a narcotic drug had been administered to the people in the house the evening before the burglary, and the accused had been there on that evening. During the proceedings before the court of petty sessions Lamb, acting as advocate for the accused, suggested that Munster might be keeping drugs at his house for immoral or criminal purposes. There was no evidence that he did so. It was held that Munster could not sue Lamb.

Not all bodies which sit to hear evidence are, however, protected by absolute privilege. For example, the following are not covered —the committee of a club, e.g. the Jockey Club. It has never been extended beyond courts of justice and tribunals acting in a manner similar to that in which the courts act.

Parliamentary Reports

By section 1 of the Parliamentary Papers Act, 1840, all reports, papers, votes, and proceedings published by the authority of Parliament are absolutely privileged. The Act protects the publication of *Hansard* but does not include the newspaper coverage of such reports. These may, however, come within the qualified privilege rules.

Newspaper Reports and Broadcasts

In certain cases absolute privilege is given by Act of Parliament. The Law of Libel Amendment Act, 1888, section 3, as amended by the Defamation Act, 1952, sections 8 and 9 (2), provides that:

> A fair and accurate report in any newspaper or by means of wireless telegraphy (as part of any programme or service provided by means of a broadcasting station within the United Kingdom) of proceedings publicly heard before any court exercising judicial authority within the United Kingdom, shall if published contemporaneously with such proceedings, be privileged: provided that nothing in this section shall authorise the publication of blasphemous or indecent matter.

The word newspaper is here defined by reference to the Newspaper Libel Registration Act, 1881, and it means "any newspaper containing public news published in England or Northern Ireland periodically at intervals not exceeding thirty-six days".

There seems to be little doubt that the words "shall be privileged" must be taken to mean absolutely privileged.

Contemporaneously

What does the word "contemporaneously" mean here? It means as nearly at the same time as the proceedings as is reasonably possible having regard to the opportunities for preparation of the report and the time of going to press or of making the broadcast. Sir Richard Webster, the then Attorney-General, said in the House of Commons that the object of inserting this clause was to prevent the raking up of old trials which might be highly disagreeable and injurious to individuals. If your daily newspaper delayed its report for ten or twelve days the report could clearly not be said to have been published contemporaneously with the proceedings.

So far as reports in newspapers or broadcasts are concerned, there are a large number of cases dealing with privilege under the common law. Journalists have a duty to the public. You cannot publish just what you like—it must be fair information on a matter of public interest.

The point to note here is that if you are reporting judicial proceedings your report must be factually accurate—especially as often in newsworthy cases evidence is given which in other circumstances would be highly defamatory. If therefore you file extraneous or incorrect reports you may render yourself virtually defenceless.

Absolute privilege does not cover headlines in a report. The headline must be factual. It must be supported by the facts to which it relates and must be reasonable having regard to the contents of the report. Nor does it cover information which you may have been able to obtain from a charge sheet if the charge sheet was not referred to in the court proceedings. An incorrect address reported may remove the protection and—most important—if you write your report in the form of an article you cannot plead successfully that you were absolutely privileged.

Under certain special circumstances trade unions and solicitors can plead privilege.

CHAPTER 9

Qualified Privilege

I. DUTY AND INTEREST

If you make libellous statements are you always liable? No. For we have seen that in certain circumstances you *are* completely protected; for example if you are a Member of Parliament speaking in the House of Commons. There are, however, a number of other occasions when you may be covered if it conforms to public policy and convenience and you have said what you believe to be the truth, making the statement honestly and without any improper or indirect motive. These occasions are of qualified privilege. How do they arise?

In many ways: such as when you make statements because you are under a duty to do so or because you are protecting your interests. You may also be covered when making reports of certain kinds.

The reason for this protection is for the common convenience and welfare of society and in these cases an absence of improper motive is essential. Chief Justice Coleridge said in 1881:

> It is better for the general good that individuals should occasionally suffer, than that freedom of communication between persons in certain relations should be in any way impeded. But the freedom of communication which it is desirous to protect is honest and kindly freedom. It is not expedient that liberty should be made the cloak of maliciousness.

Duty

What are the principles which are applied to statements made in the course of duty? The occasion is qualified if the statement

59

is fairly made by a person in the discharge of some public or private duty, whether legal or moral, or in the conduct of his own affairs, in matters where his interest is concerned. If fairly warranted by any reasonable occasion or exigency, and honestly made, such communications are protected for the common convenience and welfare of society. An occasion is privileged if you make a statement, having a moral duty to the person you address to do so, and he has an interest in receiving it. Wide publication may sometimes be privileged as the following case shows.

Wide Publication

Mr. Adam was a Member of Parliament. He had been discharged from the army for incompetence. One day in 1917 he made a speech in the House of Commons which falsely charged General Scofell, who commanded the Brigade of which his late regiment of cavalry formed part, with sending confidential reports to headquarters on officers under his command containing wilful and deliberate mis-statements. General Scofell referred the matter to the Army Council. Ward, who was its secretary, wrote a letter to him vindicating him against the charge made by Adam and containing defamatory statements about the former cavalry officer. Ward sent a copy to the Press where it was widely publicised. Adam sued Ward for libel. Ward pleaded that the letter was published on a privileged occasion. The Court held that the occasion was indeed privileged and there was no evidence of malice on the part of either the Army Council or Ward. Having regard to the circumstances under which Adam's charge was made, the publication of the libel was not unreasonably wide. In the special circumstances of the case, the defamatory statements were strictly relevant to the vindication of General Scofell and the whole of the letter was protected. Giving judgment, Lord Atkinson said:

> A privileged occasion is, in reference to qualified privilege, an occasion where the person who makes a communication has an interest or a duty, legal, social or moral to make it to the person to whom it is made. And the person to whom it is made has a corresponding interest or duty to receive it. This reciprocity is essential.

Duty and interest are involved—and interest is used in its broadest sense.

Confidences

What about statements made in answer to confidential inquiries? If your former employer is asked for a reference by your proposed new one, he is not under any legal duty to give one and you can not sue him if he will not. It is, however, his moral and social duty to state all he knows either for or against you, and if he does so honestly and without malice towards you his answer will be privileged.

If your mate is sacked and the boss tells the rest of you why he has done it, such communication may be privileged. The fact that a statement was made voluntarily does not take away privilege and there is a duty to disclose information during criminal investigations. You may be involved in inquiries about credit. It was said that everyone will admit that in carrying on the business of banking confidential inquiries are necessary with regard to the character and credit of customers applying for advances of money. In general the answer to such inquiries will be privileged. But in many instances the paid-for communications of the Mercantile Protection Associations are not. Reports from inquiry agents are usually privileged even if their language may be exaggerated.

There are certain occasions when it is your moral duty to inform Jack of certain facts about Jill, even if he has not asked you anything about it. What if she was about to announce her engagement to him and you know she is already married?

There is a duty to make statements in aid of justice, but the facts should be given in good faith to the proper authorities. Statements made by police officers in the course of their inquiries into a suspected crime are privileged.

Complaints are sometimes made against public officials—but remember that on newspaper publication no privilege will attach if a charge is given out for publication in the newspapers in advance of its delivery to the proper authority for investigation.

In *Standen* v. *S. Essex Recorder* (1934), it was held that the publication of an anonymous letter in a local newspaper commenting on the conduct of a member of a local authority at a meeting of the authority was not privileged occasion. So handle any tip-off you may get of this kind with extreme caution.

Other cases where there is a duty to pass on information arise over candidates for public office, where there is a confidential or close family relationship, clergyman and parishioner, solicitor and client. The modern tendency is to enlarge rather than restrict the scope of moral duty in such cases. It becomes much more difficult to decide when you have a duty to give information to a stranger.

So much for cases where duty is involved. Let us now turn to communications in which you and the person you write to have a common interest.

Common Interest

A communication *bona fide* made on any subject matter in which the party communicating has an interest is privileged if made to a person having a corresponding interest or duty. Here are some examples: communications between intimate friends about their doctors or servants, masters at the same school about a drunken colleague, landlord and tenant about other tenants, part-owners of a ship about the master, the president of a college to the bursar about a student, a medical superintendent to a hospital board about staff, an elector to his fellow electors at a parish meeting about the candidates.

In 1897 the Rev. Garment preached in a way which was long remembered for he was sued as a result by Mr. Goslett. So came the case which laid down that a clergyman may be under a duty to rebuke sin, but it is no part of his duty to refer in the course of his semon to any particular member of his congregation, and if he does so, no privilege will attach to his words, although they were uttered *bona fide* in the honest desire to admonish the person referred to and to warn the rest of the congregation against offending in a like manner.

Qualified Privilege of Newspapers

Section 7 of the Defamation Act, 1952, now confers qualified privilege on fair and accurate reports in newspapers. The Act has two comprehensive schedules. The first deals with statements privileged without explanation or contradiction, such as parliamentary reports, and the second schedule covers statements privileged subject to explanation or contradiction, like reports of public meetings.

Great care has to be exercised in deciding what you can print with impunity. In the case of *Simpson* v. *Downs* (1867) certain members of a town council caused to be published in a local newspaper a letter in which they charged Simpson, who was the contractor for the building of the new gaol, with serious omissions and deviations from the contract. It was held that, although such a charge would have been privileged at a council meeting, it was not in a public newspaper. Why? Because the general public, unlike the members of the town council, had no corresponding interest in the matter.

The Right to Defend

However, it has long been settled in law that where the only possible or effectual mode of discharging your duty or protecting the interest which gives rise to the privilege is to insert a notice in a public newspaper, you and the paper will be privileged.

The publication of defamatory matter in a newspaper will be privileged where the matter published is of general public interest and it is the duty of the newspaper to communicate it to the general public. The *Adam* v. *Ward* case applied here.

However, it has been held that there is no privilege attached to a newspaper which published a letter from a shareholder in a gold-mining company attacking its management and accusing directors of corruption.

To plead qualified privilege successfully, a newspaper has to show that a duty to the public was necessary. The mere fact that it was published as a matter of public news or in the *bona fide* belief that it was in the public interest will not do.

F

Chapman in 1932 sued Lord Ellesmere. He had been warned off Newmarket Heath by the Jockey Club because his horse had been drugged. The decision was published in the racing calendar and *The Times*. It was held on appeal that neither publication was privileged and that racing was not a matter of public interest sufficient to create privilege for publication in *The Times!* It should be noted that this type of case now clearly falls within the scope of section 7 of the Defamation Act, 1952.

Statements made to protect your own interests may be privileged if they are fairly made by you in the conduct of your own affairs in matters where your own interest is concerned. Obviously you have a right to reply to demands or attacks being made upon you.

An interesting case arose in 1926 when the Argus Press Ltd. published a book review by Bowen-Rowlands. They quoted a story from the book about a well-known public man who was dead, but it was not very complimentary to his daughter. She wrote a letter to them saying that the story was "pure invention from beginning to end, it is absolutely false both as to matter and manner". The newspaper published her letter without comment. Bowen-Rowlands sued, alleging that he was accused of inventing the story and telling a deliberate lie which was a reflection on him as an author. Was it?

The Court of Appeal decided that the letter, even if it was defamatory of Bowen-Rowlands, was published on a privileged occasion, for the daughter had the right to contradict the story and the newspaper to publish, and there was no evidence of malice. The newspaper won.

Controversy is an important ingredient in the lifeblood of the press. If someone is attacked in a paper, he is entitled to defend himself and retaliate. If he defames in so doing, the occasion is on the face of it privileged. This privilege is not removed by people writing anonymously.

But there are some qualifications to the right of reply in the Press. If your character is attacked you should only reply in the Press if the attack was made on you in the Press or in public. You may not be able to plead qualified privilege if you bring a private quarrel out into the open.

64

Wright wrote a book which imputed hypocrisy and gross immorality to Gladstone who was dead. Gladstone's son wrote a letter to the secretary of Wright's club calling him a liar, coward, and a foul fellow. Mr. Justice Avory in 1927 ruled that the letter was written on a privileged occasion.

Statements made to obtain redress for a grievance made in good faith can be privileged, as can statements made in reply to questions put by the person libelled. The latter case can happen when someone asks why he got the sack. But irrelevant statements are not privileged. Stick closely to the material facts.

II. REPORTS

There are a number of sources of news which can be affected by the rules governing qualified privilege. Parliamentary proceedings are one of them. Proper reports of debates in either House of Parliament are privileged, but a judge once said that a garbled or partial report, or of detached parts of proceedings published with intent to injure individuals will be disentitled to protection. Also privileged are extracts from parliamentary reports and papers. Under various Acts of Parliament certain registers have to be kept, such as records of court judgments, information under the Companies Act. Fair and accurate copies or extracts from these are privileged. This is a very old right under the common law of the country.

What is the Common Law?

The Norman kings were the first to set up a system of royal law courts covering the whole of England. The methods and rules which these courts used were the same everywhere, and became known as the common law as distinct from the old local laws or customs which varied from place to place. Later on Parliament developed and more and more statutes were passed. The common law remained, although it came to be accepted that if the common law said one thing and an Act of Parliament another, the Act must be followed. To find the common law you must look in law books, especially in the law reports, which are the actual judgments of the courts in past cases. James Derriman has written an excellent book, *Discovering the Law*, 1962. It is well worth reading as a first book on the subject.

But publication in a newspaper or by broadcasting is dealt with now under section 7 of the Defamation Act, 1952. Remember that if you publish an extract from a public document you are responsible if you do not extract or copy it correctly, and it is no answer that you have been misled by a public official. Another group is judicial proceedings. Sir Gorell Barnes, in the case of *Furniss* v. *Cambridge News Ltd.* (1907), said: "The privilege given to reports of proceedings in courts is based upon this; that as everyone cannot be in court it is for the public benefit that they should be informed of what takes place substantially as if they were present". In view of the importance to journalists of the reporting of judicial proceedings we shall consider these in some detail.

Court Proceedings

Discussion often takes place about the value of reporting court proceedings. Some say that the newspaper accounts of criminal trials put ideas into the heads of irresponsible people who may imitate the crime, thus giving rise to "carbon copy" cases. Others hold the view that publicity can be instrumental in bringing forward vital witnesses. Mr. Justice Pearson, in *The Times*, 3 June 1960, said that the main reasons for privilege in the reporting of judicial proceedings were: that the courts were open to the public; the administration of justice was a matter of public concern; the education of the public on such matters; the desirability of fair and accurate reports rather than rumours; and balancing the advantages to the public of the reporting of judicial proceedings against the detriment to individuals of being incidentally defamed.

His comments about educating the public are significant. There is a legal presumption that every man is deemed to know the law and you cannot plead ignorance of the law as a defence. Accordingly, by reporting cases accurately and in a way that the man in the street can understand, the journalist can render a most useful service to the community. Not all proceedings can be reported, nor are all reports privileged; there are exceptions provided for by statute, and, of course, if you write one, no matter how fair and accurate it is, which is immoral or seditious, you will lose the protection of qualified privilege.

Judicial proceedings are those before a properly constituted judicial tribunal exercising its jurisdiction in open court. Nearly all court proceedings are covered, but you should be careful if you are dealing with reports of proceedings in foreign countries as the protection of privilege does not always apply. It did, however, apply in the case of *Webb* v. *Times Publishing Company Ltd.* (1960), which dealt with Hume and Setty.

The Hume and Setty Case

In 1950 an English court found Hume not guilty of murder but guilty of being an accessory after the fact to murder. He went to gaol. At the trial his then wife gave evidence that she had never in her life met Setty, the murdered man. Hume was released from prison in 1958 and the *Sunday Pictorial* published an article by him in which he referred to secret meetings between his wife and Setty. As a result, his wife, by now Mrs. Webb, brought an action against the *Sunday Pictorial* which was settled in May 1959 on the terms of a statement made in open court whereby the *Sunday Pictorial* undertook not to republish passages in the article complained of by Mrs. Webb and agreed to pay her damages. The statement was published in *The Times*. In 1959 Hume was wanted by the English police on charges of attempted murder of a bank clerk and armed robbery of a bank which were alleged to have been committed by him after his release from prison. Later in 1959 he was tried by a Swiss court at Winterthur for attempted murder and armed robbery alleged to have been committed in Switzerland. In the issue of *The Times* of 25 September 1959 the following report of the proceedings before the Swiss court was published:

> Hume admits killing Setty. Body dismembered and thrown from aircraft. Winterthur, Switzerland, September 24. Hume, who is on trial on a charge of murdering a Swiss taxi driver, told the court here today that he robbed the Midland Bank in Brentford, London and shot a clerk. He also admitted killing Setty, a car dealer, out of jealousy, sawing off his limbs and making them into parcels to be dropped from an aircraft. Asked if he was married and had a child Hume replied, "Yes, but it was not mine. The father was Setty."

The report was a contemporaneous report. His former wife sued for libel, alleging that the words of the report meant that she had committed adultery with Setty and had given perjured evidence at the trial of Hume in 1950. *The Times* claimed that qualified privilege attached to the report as a fair and accurate report of foreign judicial proceedings. On a preliminary issue whether (assuming the report to be fair and accurate) the report was protected by qualified privilege it was held: the report was protected by qualified privilege because the subject matter of the report was of legitimate and proper interest to the English public as being matter much connected with the administration of justice in England, and that the reference to the father of the child being Setty, of which Mrs. Webb mainly complained, was a matter germane to Hume's confession of having killed Setty as it explained the alleged motive of jealousy and so was not extraneous matter outside the protection of the qualified privilege. (*The English and Empire Digest*, vol. 32, p. 162.)

The Whole Truth

Usually proceedings take place in open court and you should note that privilege also extends to quasi-judicial tribunals such as the proceedings of the General Medical Council. Reports must, of course, be fair and accurate. In 1936 Mitchell sued Hirst Kidd and Rennie for publishing a report headed, "Stole Motor Car" and "Motor Car Theft". The reporter present at the magistrate's court did not hear the withdrawal of the charge of theft and this was found to have been due to inattention. It was held that the report was not fair and accurate. Mitchell won his case. But you may be excused slight inaccuracies as it has been held that a report in a daily newspaper is not to be judged by the same strict standard of accuracy as a report coming from the hand of a trained lawyer, but as we have seen in the *Mitchell Case* a substantial inaccuracy will deprive the publishers of the defence of privilege.

It is very difficult indeed where proceedings are lengthy for reporters to produce abridged reports which give the essence of the case. The excellent accounts of such proceedings which are printed daily by the press come mostly from skilled and dedicated men of the highest integrity, who go to endless trouble to ensure that their reports, however condensed, do not present a garbled or false version of the case. Indeed, if they were, the possible defence of privilege would be lost. The reports must be impartial. Whatever your own views may be as a reporter, they usually have no place in a factual report of a trial. Again, beware of adding anything, even if it be true, which was not given during the proceedings. A man pleaded guilty in 1925 to assaulting a police officer in the execution of his duty. In mitigation his counsel sought to excuse his violence saying it was due to resentment against another man about whom the lawyer then used very abusive language, but whose name he did not mention. A local reporter found out who the lawyer was talking about and his name was published in a report of the case. The Court held in this Canadian case, *Geary* v. *Alger* (1925), that the report was not fair and accurate.

Great care must, of course, be taken in reporting any judgment given by the court. Where a trial lasts for some time the privilege attaches to the reports of each days' proceedings. You should not, when the case is over, pick on one particular portion of the proceedings and report that if the effect is to make it unfair. Remember that both the heading and the report must be read together. The heading must be a fair index of the matter. Facts and comments should be clearly separated. Often the documents produced in all or part of the proceedings are of special interest to the reporter, but care should be taken in dealing with those which are not brought up in open court. Reports must not be published maliciously. In the case of *Morrison* v. *News of the World*, which is reported in *The Times*, 17 May 1929, an over-enthusiastic journalist wrote an account of a trial, but part of the report was a description not only of what he heard and saw in court but also of the plaintiff's house, the character of his friends, the crowd which gathered to see him, and much more. Mr. Justice Swift held the article could not be defended as a report of judicial proceedings.

Newspaper Defences

Section 7 of the Defamation Act, 1952, says that if you publish in a newspaper a report dealing with a matter set out in the schedule, you shall be privileged unless your publication is proved to be made with malice.

If you are sued for libel in respect of the publication of any such report as is mentioned in Part II of the Schedule to the Defamation Act, 1952, the provisions of section 7 (which I am now quoting) shall *not* be a defence for you if it is proved that you had been requested by the plaintiff to publish in the newspaper, in which the original publication was made, a reasonable letter or statement by way of explanation or contradiction, and you have refused or neglected to do so, or you have done so in a manner not adequate or not reasonable, having regard to all the circumstances [section 7 (11) and (12)]. So qualified privilege can depend on you being asked to make amends and doing so satisfactorily.

You cannot be protected by section 7 (3) for publishing anything prohibited by law or not of public concern or which is not for the public benefit.

Section 7 (4) says that nothing in this Act shall affect subsisting privileges. The Act goes on to define "newspaper" as follows: "any paper containing public news or observations thereon, or consisting wholly or mainly of advertisements, which is printed for sale and is published in the United Kingdom either periodically or in parts or numbers at intervals not exceeding thirty-six days" [section 7 (5)].

Broadcasting

There used to be considerable discussion as to the place of broadcasting in all this, and the question is now firmly resolved by section 9 which says that so far as section 3 of the Parliamentary Papers Act, 1840, is concerned, the reference to printing included a reference to broadcasting by means of wireless telegraphy. There follows a comprehensive section 9 (2) which provides that section 7 of the 1952 Act and section 3 of the 1888 Act as amended shall apply to broadcast reports of any station within the United Kingdom, and it shall have the effect, in relation to any such broadcasting: as if the words "in the newspaper in which" is to be read as "in the manner in which"—which is the lawyer's way of saying that for newspaper reports you can read broadcast reports.

What about the broadcasting stations? These are much in the news these days, particularly over the pirate and local stations. Here it means any station licensed by the Postmaster-General. We have already seen that Part I of the Schedule to the Defamation Act gives a list of seven types of statements which are privileged without explanation or contradiction. Part II deals with statements which are privileged subject to explanation or contradiction, for that is what qualified privilege can mean. I give a synopsis below, but you should read the full Act carefully. It is set out at the end of this book.

Associations

The eight items of the Schedule are concerned with associations. You may be protected if you make a fair and accurate report of the work of any of the following associations, its committees, or governing body thereof:

(a) associations formed in the United Kingdom for art, science, religion, or learning;
(b) associations formed in the United Kingdom for promoting or safeguarding the interests of any trade, business, industry, or profession;

(c) associations formed in the United Kingdom for promoting or safeguarding the interests of any game, sport, or pasttime.

Meetings

Item 9 of the Schedule covers meetings. You may invoke privilege if you give a fair and accurate report of the proceedings at any *bona fide* and lawfully public meeting held in the United Kingdom for the furtherance or discussion of any matter of public concern, whether the admission to the meeting is general or restricted. The tenth item of the Schedule deals with special kinds of meetings, viz:

(a) local authorities;
(b) Justices of the peace acting otherwise than as a court;
(c) parliamentary, royal, or ministerial commissions, tribunals, committees, or inquiries;
(d) local inquiries;
(e) statutory tribunals, boards, or committees.

Of course, if the meeting is in private, privilege does not arise, for it is a condition that the above, for you to be protected, must not be meetings or sittings, admission to which is denied to representatives of newspapers and other members of the press.

Items 11 and 12 cover company meetings, and fair and accurate reports of matter issued for the information of the public by government departments, offices of state, local authorities, or chief officers of police.

There are many interesting cases on what the Act means. Would you think that a student meeting to commemorate a statesman not confined to the organising body is a public meeting? You would probably say yes, and you would be correct. Watch your step in reporting protest meetings. They can so easily become unlawful by obstructing the highway or be likely to lead to a breach of the peace, and if the meeting is not lawful, your privilege protection vanishes.

In addition to courts of law there are a number of tribunals and bodies exercising discipline and providing good copy for the papers. Local authorities have many meetings which are of considerable interest to the public. Have you as a journalist a right to be present? And if you are allowed in, are there any restrictions on what you can publish? We have seen that you can report a criminal or civil trial with impunity if you give contemporaneously a fair and accurate report of proceedings heard in public in court, for your writing will be privileged. That then is the position regarding the courts. But what of other meetings like those of local authorities? Here only qualified privilege is given. The right of the Press to attend meetings of local authorities is governed by the Public Bodies (Admissions to Meetings) Act, 1960. It enables the Press and other members of the public to be admitted to all meetings of the authority and its committees, but both can be temporarily excluded by resolution if the nature of the business makes it in the public interest to do so. To do so a special resolution must be passed so that exclusion of the Press can only take place whenever publicity would be prejudicial to the public interest by reason of the confidential nature of the business to be transacted, or for other special reason stated in the resolution and arising from the nature of that business or of the proceedings. Public notice must be given of each meeting and copies of the agenda supplied on request and payment of postage to any newspaper or news agency. The agenda need not include matters which are likely to be debated in private. An agenda of and a fair and accurate report of the proceedings of any local authority enjoys qualified privilege, provided that it is not a meeting, admission to which is denied to newspaper representatives and the public. Defamation Act, 1952, section 7 and Schedule, Public Bodies (Admission to Meetings) Act, 1960, sections 1 (5)–2 (1).

Fair and Accurate Reports

As to what is a fair and accurate report, whatever you write, however carefully or ably you write, everyone will have his or her own opinion as to whether what you wrote is fair and accurate. You can only do your honest best. People become so emotionally involved in matters with which they are concerned that it is very difficult for them to look back objectively on what was said or done. Listen to a man telling his friends what he said at a meeting, and if you were present you may be quite surprised at the version he gives. But this is human nature. We all like to think we are pretty good, and that we matter, and consequently what we say matters. This is where the cool detachment of the reporter is of supreme importance.

Anyway, whether your report is fair and accurate is a question of fact to be considered afresh in each individual case. But if you are challenged you will have to prove that it is. We have seen there is no need for the report to be accurate down to the last detail, although it helps if it is. A few slight inaccuracies will not deprive it of protection, but they must be slight. What about the things you left out? This is something which always upsets the man reported. And you must be prepared for this ever-recurring situation. The answer is that you are the reporter and you must make up your own mind as to what is important from a reporting point of view. The speaker cannot do this although he will often try to help you by press handouts, releases with embargoes, and advance texts of speeches. Incidentally, treat the latter with caution. So many speakers give you a splendid release and then go on to say something quite different. You must check the release against the actual speech delivered. What is the legal test on omissions? Where the omission would have made an appreciable difference in favour of the speaker reported, or have counteracted an objectionable statement in the report, you would probably be held at fault with your report and your possible defence of qualified privilege would be of no avail. Much is written piously by journalists of their view that what they do is of public concern and public benefit. And, indeed, so it is. But remember it does not always follow that because the public are interested in a matter it is for their benefit that such a report should be published. It is not enough to prove that the meeting, proceedings, and much of the speeches were all for the public benefit. You must prove that the publication of the actual words complained of was for the public benefit. This often places editors in positions of considerable difficulty. The rule is, however, quite clear and designed to prevent scurrilous attacks made with the object of publicity being given further circulation by newspapers, who would otherwise simply excuse themselves by pleading privilege.

CHAPTER 10

Other Defences

WE SHALL now deal with some of the other defences which may be available to you.

Apology

If you libel someone and then say you are sorry your regret is not a defence. It can, however, materially affect the amount of damages you may be called upon to pay. The person you have libelled is not bound to accept your apology but he cannot stop you bringing the offer forward in mitigation of damages. It is the offer which matters in this situation. You should, however, be careful not to rush in with an apology unless you are quite sure of all the facts. An apology could even result in the matter being aggravated.

Apology and Payment into Court

Before the passing of the Defamation Act, 1952, there was a special defence open to newspapers and periodicals under Lord Campbell's Libel Act of 1843. You could, if you had no better defence, plead an apology and pay a sum of money into court by way of amends. You would still have to prove that there was no malice or negligence in publication. This procedure is not used very often nowadays as it is highly technical and difficult.

Unintentional Defamation

You have learnt that if you libel someone you are liable and that it is no defence for you to plead that you did not intend to libel anyone and that you had been careful. This was very much the position up to 1952 but section 4 of the Defamation Act brought about a very important change.

This section deals with cases where the defamation is unintentional and protects you where the statements complained of were published by you innocently in relation to the plaintiff. First you must make an "offer of amends". This, as we shall see, does not mean an offer of money. If the offer is accepted no proceedings for defamation can be taken against you. The way in which the offer has to be made is clearly laid down. It has, incidentally, to be accompanied by an affidavit specifying the facts you rely on.

If the person attacked does not accept your offer, then if you are sued it can be a defence for you to prove that the words were published innocently and that the offer was made as soon as practicable and that the offer has not been withdrawn.

But what does "publish innocently" mean? It applies if the following conditions are satisfied:

(a) You did not intend to publish [the words] of and concerning the other person and
You did not know of circumstances by virtue of which they might be understood to refer to him; OR

(b) The words were not defamatory on the face of them, and you did not know of circumstances by virtue of which they might be understood to be defamatory of the complainant. [Section 5.]

Offer of Amends

Where the words are deemed to be published innocently you may make an offer of amends. You must make your offer specifically under section 4 of the Act and it must be accompanied by an affidavit setting out the facts you rely on, showing that the words in question were published by you innocently. No further evidence in defence under this section can be given other than evidence of facts specified in the affidavit. The offer of amends means:

(a) In any case, to publish or join in the publication of a suitable correction of the words complained of, and a sufficient apology to the party aggrieved by those words;
(b) where copies of the libel have been distributed by or with your knowledge you will take reasonable steps to notify those concerned that a libel is alleged.

If your offer is accepted and is performed, no proceedings can be taken against you, as the publisher, by the person aggrieved.

Disputes over fulfilment are to be referred to the High Court, whose decision is final. If the offer is not accepted, then you may have a defence under the procedure outlined above if you prove that you published innocently and that the offer was made as soon as practicable after you were notified of the alleged libel and that the offer is still open.

Authorised Publication—Release

There is an old Latin maxim: *volenti non fit injuria*—a volunteer cannot sue if injured. How does this arise in libel? A criminal may agree with you to let you have his memoirs. He supplies all the information and material and in due course you publish them. On reflection he may prefer not to have authorised publication. He cannot sue you even if his reputation has undoubtedly suffered as a result of the articles, for the law will not uphold claims by people who authorised or consented to the acts of which they complain.

Statute of Limitation

Even if someone has got the right to sue you over a libel you have published they cannot let the matter rest indefinitely and then suddenly start proceedings many years after the incident. This rule applies to all kinds of actions as well as to libel, and it is governed chiefly by the Limitation Act, 1939. Actions which are actionable without proof of special damage such as for libel must be brought within six years from the date of publication. Actions where special damage has to be proved must be brought within six years of the date when the damage was sustained.

If, however, the person you have attacked is under a disability, e.g. an infant, or a convict, or of unsound mind, time does not start to run until he is free of the disability.

Res Judicata—Previous Court Action

Another defence you may have and which has to be considered very carefully by your legal adviser is whether the person attacked has already brought an action against you for the publication of the same words. Even although the words complained of are the same, yet if they appear in a different publication the person attacked has a fresh cause of action. The position of news collecting agencies is curious. They may be liable twice—once for passing on the libel, and again jointly with each paper that publishes it.

Death

Finally, if the person about whom you have published a libel dies, that will usually be the end of the matter. The reason for this is because the law regards this type of case as being a personal one to the persons concerned, and reputation in this sense means the esteem in which living people are held. But if you slander goods the right to sue can survive. Your own death may affect the position if you are being sued personally. It may not if your employers are being sued.

These then are the defences to an action for defamation.

Now let us consider who can sue.

G

CHAPTER 11

Who Can Sue?

Parties to an Action

Special rules govern actions involving ambassadors, foreign statesmen, convicts, foreign subjects, bankrupts, infants, lunatics, drunks, married women, representatives of dead people, corporations at home and abroad, firms, trade unions, organisations, societies, and masters and servants. We will deal here with the last example.

Employers

Your master is liable for defamatory words published by you with his authority or consent or if, in doing what is complained of, you were acting in the scope of your authority, i.e. in the course of an employment which is authorised.

"The proprietor of a newspaper is civilly liable for any libel it publishes, even though published while he was away without his knowledge and contrary to his orders." Why? The editor is his employee and it is within the scope of the editor's authority to send to the printers anything he thinks ought to be published. His liability is not upon the ground of his being the publisher, but because he is responsible for the acts of the actual publisher. Similarly, the printer and publisher are his agents to print and publish whatever matter the editor sends them. (*Gatley on Libel and Slander*, 6th edn., p. 402.)

Lord Tenterden summed it up as far back as 1829 in the case
of *R. v. Gutch* when he said:

> Surely a person who derives profit from and who furnishes means for
> carrying on the concern, and entrusts the conduct of the publication
> to one whom he selects, and in whom he confides, may be said to cause
> to be published what actually appears, and ought to be answerable
> although you cannot show that he was individually concerned in the
> particular publication.

If I write a libellous letter and send it to your editor I shall be
liable for the resulting damage. If I give you libellous information,
knowing you intend to write an article on it, I shall be liable even
though you may have asked me for information and I did not
request publication. If I give you a copy of a libellous speech to
publish and you do so, you will be my agent and I shall be responsible, possibly alone, provided you have acted in good faith. But
I may not be liable if you alter my copy substantially. There are
special considerations where you are dealing with translators.

Employees

Malice on the part of a servant or agent may affect the liability
of the employer, depending upon whether the occasion was
privileged. It is wise to remember that as a general rule every
person who publishes a libel is personally liable, for, as Lord
Moulton said in the case of *Vacher* v. *London Society of Com-
positors* in 1913: "It is a fundamental principle of English law
that no tortfeasor can excuse himself from the consequences of
his acts by setting up that he was acting only as the agent of
another." So if you are in employment and you do not know how
you stand in your own firm over these matters, the sooner you
inquire discreetly the better.

Contempt of Court

All superior courts have the right to punish you if they judge
you to be guilty of contempt of court. What is contempt of court?

It is of two kinds, civil and criminal. It can be either (a) words or acts obstructing or calculated to obstruct the administration of justice, or (b) contempt in procedure by disobeying an order of the court or judge. Where any insult or open defiance is offered in the face of the court, the offence is treated as a contempt of court and is punishable at once. In such a case the judge may order a fine or imprisonment or both. A man who threw tomatoes at two appeal judges in 1938 went to gaol for six weeks. There is no trial by jury. It is up to the judge to decide, but nowadays you can appeal. Incidentally, jurors eating in court have been held guilty of contempt. What happens if you are sent to gaol? Generally speaking, you stay there until you have "purged your contempt"—that is, until you have satisfied the court that you are truly repentant. You can be "attached", which means arrested on the order of a judge.

If you publish the photograph of a man charged with a criminal offence when the identity of the accused might be in question, you may commit a contempt. You have probably noticed that the police usually cover up the heads and faces of the accused with sacks or coats. This may keep everyone out of trouble. You must be very careful NOT to take any photographs within the precincts of the court—not even of men with coats over their heads being bundled along near the entrance before or after a trial. The Attorney-General in 1967 issued a special memorandum drawing the attention of editors to this. Note also that a caption of a news film suggesting that an accused man has committed the offence is contempt. [*R.* v. *Hutchinson ex parte McMahon* (1936).]

In 1924 the *Evening Standard* and *Daily Express* were held to be in contempt for allowing its reporters to act as amateur detectives when a man had been arrested on a criminal charge and publishing accounts of their investigations. In the case of a newspaper the order may be made against the proprietor, publisher, editor, author, or printer. What happens if you are in the middle of a crime story and you hear that a suspect has been arrested? The story may have to be stopped at once. This can give rise to some difficulty if the first account has already appeared in earlier editions.

There is no privilege known to the law by which a journalist can refuse to answer a question which is relevant to an inquiry and is one which, in the opinion of the judge, it is proper for him to be asked. So said Lord Justice Donovan in the case brought by the Attorney-General against Mulholland and Foster—two journalists who refused before a tribunal set up under the Tribunals of Inquiry (Evidence) Act, 1921, to name or describe the sources of information in articles written by them which the chairman of the tribunal certified were relevant to the inquiry. One of the journalists was sentenced to six and the other to three months' imprisonment for contempt. (*The Times*, 7 March 1963; *Current Law* 2768.)

Criminal Libel

What you publish may be so provocative that it tends to provoke the person you write about to commit a breach of the peace. This is a public offence. So libel, in addition to being a civil wrong, can also be a crime. It is punishable with a fine or imprisonment. Prosecutions are very rare. At common law truth was never accepted in itself as a defence to proceedings for *criminal* libel, hence the curiously worded maxim "The greater the truth, the greater the libel". No criminal proceedings can be commenced against the proprietor of a newspaper for any libel he may be alleged to have published without the order of a judge. The matter should concern the general interests of the public.

Libel on the Dead

As damage to the plaintiff's reputation is the essence of civil proceedings for defamation, an action claiming damages for libel or slander does not lie in respect of defamation of a dead person.

Naturally, though, the position is different if the defamation of a dead person contains by implication an attack upon the living. If I say "Poor old Mrs. X who died last week was never married at all—she lived in adultery all her life", this implies that the

83

children of Mrs. X are bastards and they certainly can sue me (assuming, of course, that it is untrue) for damages.

A libel on a dead person is not a criminal offence unless it can be clearly shown to have caused injury or annoyance to the living. Criminal proceedings may be taken for a libel on a dead man if the natural consequence is to provoke his family to a breach of the peace, or if it can be proved that it was published with the intention of provoking or injuring his living descendants.

Blasphemy

Blasphemy is profane speaking of God or sacred things— impious reference. If you publish an article ridiculing or vilifying God or Christianity or the Bible in general with intent to insult and shock those who believe, or if your intention was to pervert or mislead the ignorant, you may be guilty of the criminal libel offence of blasphemy. Your intention is the crux of the matter. Times change and much greater freedom of expression is permitted nowadays. Views are freely expressed at present which a few hundred years ago would certainly have resulted in imprisonment. What about religious argument and controversy? These are not blasphemous if they are conducted decently and the views put forward, however extreme, are proferred honestly. Several television and radio programmes demonstrate this in no uncertain way. Much depends on whether the argument was in public or in private. It is the form of expression which is so closely examined, not the content. If you advance your views by way of scurrilous attacks or irreverent language which would shock or outrage the feelings of believers, you may be guilty of blasphemy.

Seditious Libel

A seditious libel is one which tends to degrade or vilify the Constitution, the Sovereign, the Government, Parliament, promote insurrection, create discontent through its members, impugn corruption to judges or the administration of justice, or to excite people otherwise than by lawful means, to raise discontent or

84

disaffection, to promote feelings of ill-will and hostility between different classes of subject.

Blackmailing Actions

There are certain people who regard newspapers as fair game for a lawsuit. They take the slightest opportunity, use the flimsiest pretext of making a claim upon a publisher alleging that they have been libelled. The chances of their succeeding in their action may be remote. That does not prevent them instructing a solicitor to make a claim or subsequently issuing a writ. Often it is quite apparent, even on a superficial examination of the circumstances, that they have not in fact been libelled, that no one could really believe that they were.

The Defamation Act has done a certain amount to put an end to this kind of speculative litigation, but it still persists. You may find a story that you have written accurately and well seized upon by one of these leeches as the basis for a claim. You know it is spurious, your editor knows it, and your lawyer knows it. Why then worry? Fight the case, you are bound to win. True enough, but the snag here is that to fight the case might cost hundreds or, indeed, thousands of pounds, whereas the specious plaintiff might be quite prepared to settle for fifty! This presents a difficult question to the proprietors. The easy way out is, of course, to pay up. This is quite wrong morally, however much better it may be financially. People talk. And if it becomes known that a particular paper is good for a "soft touch"—believe me, they will get plenty of claims. The only way is to be tough and stand firm. This, too, becomes known and the number of blackmailing claims will diminish. It is up to you to see that your copy is so good and so accurate that if this unfortunate situation ever arises with you, your paper will back you with confidence and not settle because there is a slight doubt about the story you have written.

The editors of the sixth edition of *Gatley on Libel and Slander* (1967)—the leading textbook on defamation—wrote in their preface, "All trials are longer than they used to be, and defamation actions have, if anything, a worse record than others." While

85

proceedings are unpredictably expensive (a number of recent long cases have ended in one or more disagreements by the jury), both the pressure that can be exerted by a gold-digging plaintiff and the anxiety that must be felt by a plaintiff with a good case faced by a defendant with a long pocket are increased. So keep your journalism at the highest possible standard of accuracy and integrity.

Keeping Inside the Law

Editing

How does a newspaper keep inside the law? This is a difficult matter and calls for great knowledge and judgment. The problem is all the more complex because of the speed at which papers are published. The first check on legality is with the reporter himself. An experienced reporter should know enough of the elements of the law to avoid the more obvious pitfalls. The next is with the sub-editor or editor who deals with his copy. If the eagle eye of the newsroom has overlooked some doubtful point, the copy taster, or sub-editor, must initiate inquiry by a reporter or one of the experts of the staff. He must also watch for possible libels or contempt of court in copy and, if in doubt, refer these to the editor or the legal adviser. On a national newspaper the full staff of sub-editors numbers twenty or more, headed by the chief sub-editor. The night editor joins them to direct proceedings at crucial moments, and in some offices a legal adviser is present as well to deal with problems which may crop up at a moment's notice. National papers have a night lawyers' roster which ensures that a skilled legal adviser is always at hand if needed. Not all the lawyers are, however, in full-time employment with the paper concerned. Often they are experienced solicitors or barristers who work on a part-time basis.

Proof Reading

Proof readers, too, have a special responsibility in ensuring the accuracy of what is printed. They are chosen for their specialised and expert knowledge and sound judgment. Theirs is primarily the art and practice of finding mistakes in printed matter before publication and of indicating the needed corrections. They may spot a libel or think they have. In either case it is important that the matter shall be queried and passed back to editorial authority.

Clanger Corner

Many offices have their "Clanger Corner" with the howlers stuck up on the wall, and not a few of them are examples of insult, ridicule, or *double entendre*. Read them whenever and wherever you can.

Unlawful Publications

There are many things which it is unlawful to publish—for example, indecent matter or medical or surgical details which, if published, would be calculated to injure public morals, certain divorce case details, matrimonial proceedings, cases involving children, official secrets, replicas of bank notes and stamps, certain advertisements dealing with specified diseases, obscene matter, details of particular medicines and food and drugs, lotteries, financial matters.

There are a great many Acts, rules and regulations, orders, codes of standards and standard conditions, and forms of contract dealing with them. Journalism and advertising are close to each other in these matters. The best book on the subject is *Modern Advertising Law*, by Peter Langdon-Davies.

Checking the Story

Where news has come in from a reputable source such as the Press Association—Reuters, a certain amount of sifting and checking for accuracy will already have been done. The chief sub-editor engaged in "make-up" also has a special responsibility.

No matter how carefully the pages have been planned there is always more news and more type than they will hold, for to be short of type would be disastrous. At this stage and with little time to spare the make-up sub-editor has to act quickly but carefully so that the report is not marred. He must not cut out points mentioned in the headlines or crossheads. What he cuts out can be of vital importance in deciding the question of libel liability. Your story as filed may have been quite correct, but the omission of a paragraph in printing could give the report a totally different aspect and make it much harder to withstand a claim. So make-up is not just a question of style and attractive layout; above all, the fullest report of the truth must still be the guideline.

In a provincial paper the same care is taken to ensure accuracy, although there may not be the same number of people employed; the accent may be on local affairs and varying use will be made of agency copy.

But you will now see that from the moment you start to write your story until the time it is being sold on the streets, quite a number of keen eyes backed with years of experience will have scanned your report to make sure it does not infringe the laws of defamation. You can do a great deal to help them by learning as much as you can about the legal limits of journalism so that you keep within them.

Night Lawyer in the *U.K. Press Gazette* recently wrote:

> Sometimes however people who find themselves on duty at holiday time are juniors. They may be unwilling or unable to seek the guidance of their more experienced colleagues. They may find people with whom they could check details difficult to reach because they are not at work or have gone away from home for the holiday. In provincial offices especially there will be people holding the fort in the familiar way. A young reporter may do the police calls and tour the hospitals with the mayor, and check the fire stations and hospitals all alone for a day or two. He may cover the court where the drunks appear and go to an inquest on some domestic or road tragedy. He may pick up a story with a funny or seasonal or pathetic angle. He will have plenty to do, all alone in the office. Perhaps he would not have appreciated the implication or inaccuracy which might have crept into his copy. When it is left for those who come on duty afterwards he may not be around to answer enquiries. If it gets into print the damage is done.

It is hoped that this book will help you to avoid this kind of situation—one in which we can so easily find ourselves.

New Laws

On 1 January 1968 a new Criminal Justice Act came into force which affects journalists.

Section 1 provides for automatic committal for trial without hearing evidence where it is all in written statements and the defendant is represented. Section 2 imposes the conditions on receiving such statements in evidence.

Section 3 starts on Press provisions. It makes it unlawful to publish in Great Britain a report of committal proceedings except for the details allowed by subsection 4.

But the ban will be lifted on the application of any defendant, and if the magistrates decide not to commit for trial the committal hearing can be reported. The committal hearing can also be reported if anyone wants to after the trial of the last defendant is over.

Where the magistrates turn the preliminary examination into a summary trial for one or more but not all of several defendants, but commit others for trial, it will be lawful to publish the proceedings up to the change as well as after.

Subsection 4 tells you what you can give in a report of committal proceedings.

You may identify the court and give the names of the examining magistrates. About the parties (i.e. the defendant and complainant) and the witnesses you may report their names, addresses, and occupations. Of the defendants and the witnesses you may state their ages. Since the actual complaint is most often going to be laid by a policeman and you can get his age if you want it, the distinction is puzzling. The word "parties" is doubtless used to cover private prosecutions which are uncommon.

You may set out the offences with which the defendants are charged or a summary of them. You may report the names of counsel and solicitors engaged in the case.

The decision of the court is reportable. You can give the committal for trial or the decision to commit some but not others of the defendants, and the decision on the disposal of defendants not committed.

Of those actually committed you may state the charges, or a summary of them, on which they are committed, and the court to which they are committed.

If, as so often happens, the hearing before the examining magistrates is adjourned, you may report the date and place of the next hearing. You may also report any arrangements as to bail on adjournment, or committal, and whether legal aid was granted to the defendants. Under subsection 5, if the limits are exceeded, proprietor, editor, or publisher of the newspaper or periodical which publishes it is guilty of an offence.

If a written report of the proceedings is published otherwise than as part of a newspaper or periodical, the person who publishes it is guilty of an offence. Here is a possible danger for news agency men or freelances sending out reports to customers not for publication in the paper but for background information. That could be a technical publication and make the freelance liable to conviction.

Any member of the public could sit in court and repeat such information *viva voce* and not commit an offence.

The act applies to broadcasts and the maximum penalty for a breach is £500. Prosecution must have the consent of the Attorney-General.

The Clerk of the Court must post up certain notices, and reports published as soon as practicable shall be deemed to be contemporaneous.

The above is a *U.K. Press Gazette* summary.

CHAPTER 12

Scotland

THE legal limits to journalism dealt with in this book refer to the law of England and Wales and not to Scotland. There are a good many differences. In Scotland the police do not act as prosecutors. This is done by Crown officers, chiefly the Procurator Fiscal, who usually carries out preliminary inquiries in private. A verdict of "not proven" can be brought in by the jury (15 people) at a criminal trial, or they can bring in a majority verdict which is now part of English law. Magistrates in Scotland are appointed by the town council and most criminal cases are heard in the sheriff court. Appeals lie to the Appeal Court of the High Court of Justiciary; barristers are known as advocates; solicitors use the initials S.S.C.—Solicitors of the Supreme Court. The Scottish courts have similar powers to the English courts to exclude the Press or the public if they consider it to be in the interests of justice. There are no coroners' courts in Scotland and the sheriff court does the work of the county court. Bankruptcy procedure is quite different. So far as admission of the Press to public meetings is concerned, the position in Scotland is broadly similar to that in England and Wales; the public bodies are listed in the Public Bodies Act, 1960.

There is no provision in Scottish law that a boy under fourteen years of age cannot be guilty of rape. The rules relating to contempt and privilege have general application to Scotland. The Defamation Act, 1952, has a general application to Scotland, but sections 1, 2, 8, and 13 apply only to England. There is no technical distinction in Scottish law between libel and slander. Slander is deemed to be a statement which is false, defamatory, and malicious. The plaintiff in an action is called the pursuer.

The foregoing is set out merely to signpost some of the differences between the two systems of law. If you have an assignment over the border you will find that the general rules of sound reporting apply, but you would be well advised to seek expert advice in Scottish law if in doubt at any time. L. C. J. McNae, former head of the Press Association's Special Reporting Service and one of the leading authorities on Press Law—the editor of *Essential Law for Journalists* (1964)—draws attention in it to a number of distinctions drafted by E. Rosslyn Mitchell and W. L. Taylor, both of Glasgow and both with traditions of legal work for the press in Scotland.

CHAPTER 13

Conclusions

WE HAVE been concerned principally with the legal limits of journalism. Many people like to keep their activities private—but it may be journalists duty to make them public. What about the long-term view? What makes a good journalist? He is the eyes and ears of the paper—with an immense range of interests. He has the highest standards of probity, tact, discretion, wide general knowledge, a love of his fellow men, sympathy, understanding, and a sense of humour. He has the skill to see and record effectively, accurately, and legally. According to the way you do this, so is the reputation of all journalism in your hands.

Appendix
Defamation Act, 1952

15 & 16 Geo. 6 & 1 Eliz. 2   Ch. 66*

Arrangement of Sections

Section

*Reproduced by kind permission of Her Majesty's Stationery Office.

CHAPTER 66

An Act to amend the law relating to libel and slander and other malicious falsehoods. (30th October 1952.)

BE it enacted by the Queen's most Excellent Majesty, by and with the advice and consent of the Lords Spiritual and Temporal, and Commons, in this present Parliament assembled, and by the authority of the same, as follows:—

Broadcast statements

1. For the purposes of the law of libel and slander, the broadcasting of words by means of wireless telegraphy shall be treated as publication in permanent form.

Slander affecting official, professional or business reputation

2. In an action for slander in respect of words calculated to disparage the plaintiff in any office, profession, calling, trade or business held or carried on by him at the time of the publication, it shall not be necessary to allege or prove special damage, whether or not the words are spoken of the plaintiff in the way of his office, profession, calling, trade or business.

Slander of title, &c.

3.—(1) In an action for slander of title, slander of goods or other malicious falsehood, it shall not be necessary to allege or prove special damage—

(a) if the words upon which the action is founded are calculated to cause pecuniary damage to the plaintiff and are published in writing or other permanent form; or

(b) if the said words are calculated to cause pecuniary damage to the plaintiff in respect of any office, profession, calling, trade or business held or carried on by him at the time of the publication.

(2) Section one of this Act shall apply for the purposes of this section as it applies for the purposes of the law of libel and slander.

Unintentional defamation

4.—(1) A person who has published words alleged to be defamatory of another person may, if he claims that the words were published by him innocently in relation to that other person, make an offer of amends under this section; and in any such case—

(*a*) if the offer is accepted by the party aggrieved and is duly performed, no proceedings for libel or slander shall be taken or continued by that party against the person making the offer in respect of the publication in question (but without prejudice to any cause of action against any other person jointly responsible for that publication);

(*b*) if the offer is not accepted by the party aggrieved, then, except as otherwise provided by this section, it shall be a defence, in any proceedings by him for libel or slander against the person making the offer in respect of the publication in question, to prove that the words complained of were published by the defendant innocently in relation to the plaintiff and that the offer was made as soon as practicable after the defendant received notice that they were or might be defamatory of the plaintiff, and has not been withdrawn.

(2) An offer of amends under this section must be expressed to be made for the purposes of this section, and must be accompanied by an affidavit specifying the facts relied upon by the person making it to show that the words in question were published by him innocently in relation to the party aggrieved; and for the purposes of a defence under paragraph (*b*) of subsection (1) of this section no evidence, other than evidence of facts specified in the affidavit, shall be admissible on behalf of that person to prove that the words were so published.

(3) An offer of amends under this section shall be understood to mean an offer—

(a) in any case, to publish or join in the publication of a suitable correction of the words complained of, and a sufficient apology to the party aggrieved in respect of those words;

(b) where copies of a document or record containing the said words have been distributed by or with the knowledge of the person making the offer, to take such steps as are reasonably practicable on his part for notifying persons to whom copies have been so distributed that the words are alleged to be defamatory of the party aggrieved.

(4) Where an offer of amends under this section is accepted by the party aggrieved—

(a) any question as to the steps to be taken in fulfilment of the offer as so accepted shall in default of agreement between the parties be referred to and determined by the High Court, whose decision thereon shall be final;

(b) the power of the court to make orders as to costs in proceedings by the party aggrieved against the person making the offer in respect of the publication in question, or in proceedings in respect of the offer under paragraph (a) of this subsection, shall include power to order the payment by the person making the offer to the party aggrieved of costs on an indemnity basis and any expenses reasonably incurred or to be incurred by that party in consequence of the publication in question;

and if no such proceedings as aforesaid are taken, the High Court may, upon application made by the party aggrieved, make any such order for the payment of such costs and expenses as aforesaid as could be made in such proceedings.

(5) For the purposes of this section words shall be treated as published by one person (in this subsection referred to as the

APPENDIX. DEFAMATION ACT, 1952

publisher) innocently in relation to another person if and only if the following conditions are satisfied, that is to say—

(a) that the publisher did not intend to publish them of and concerning that other person, and did not know of circumstances by virtue of which they might be understood to refer to him; or

(b) that the words were not defamatory on the face of them, and the publisher did not know of circumstances by virtue of which they might be understood to be defamatory of that other person.

and in either case that the publisher exercised all reasonable care in relation to the publication; and any reference in this subsection to the publisher shall be construed as including a reference to any servant or agent of his who was concerned with the contents of the publication.

(6) Paragraph (b) of subsection (1) of this section shall not apply in relation to the publication by any person of words of which he is not the author unless he proves that the words were written by the author without malice.

Justification

5. In an action for libel or slander in respect of words containing two or more distinct charges against the plaintiff, a defence of justification shall not fail by reason only that the truth of every charge is not proved if the words not proved to be true do not materially injure the plaintiff's reputation having regard to the truth of the remaining charges.

Fair comment

6. In an action for libel or slander in respect of words consisting partly of allegations of fact and partly of expression of opinion, a defence of fair comment shall not fail by reason only that the truth of every allegation of fact is not proved if the expression of opinion is fair comment having regard to such of

the facts alleged or referred to in the words complained of as are proved.

Qualified privilege of newspapers

7.—(1) Subject to the provisions of this section, the publication in a newspaper of any such report or other matter as is mentioned in the Schedule to this Act shall be privileged unless the publication is proved to be made with malice.

(2) In an action for libel in respect of the publication of any such report or matter as is mentioned in Part II of the Schedule to this Act, the provisions of this section shall not be a defence if it is proved that the defendant has been requested by the plaintiff to publish in the newspaper in which the original publication was made a reasonable letter or statement by way of explanation or contradiction, and has refused or neglected to do so, or has done so in a manner not adequate or not reasonable having regard to all the circumstances.

(3) Nothing in this section shall be construed as protecting the publication of any matter the publication of which is prohibited by law, or of any matter which is not of public concern and the publication of which is not for the public benefit.

(4) Nothing in this section shall be construed as limiting or abridging any privilege subsisting (otherwise than by virtue of section four of the Law of Libel Amendment Act, 1888) immediately before the commencement of this Act.

(5) In this section the expression "newspaper" means any paper containing public news or observations thereon, or consisting wholly or mainly of advertisements, which is printed for sale and is published in the United Kingdom either periodically or in parts or numbers at intervals not exceeding thirty-six days.

Extent of Law of Libel Amendment Act, 1888, s.3

8. Section three of the Law of Libel Amendment Act, 1888 (which relates to contemporary reports of proceedings before courts exercising judicial authority) shall apply and apply only to courts exercising judicial authority within the United Kingdom.

Extension of certain defences to broadcasting

9.—(1) Section three of the Parliamentary Papers Act, 1840 (which confers protection in respect of proceedings for printing extracts from or abstracts of parliamentary papers) shall have effect as if the reference to printing included a reference to broadcasting by means of wireless telegraphy.

(2) Section seven of this Act and section three of the Law of Libel Amendment Act, 1888, as amended by this Act shall apply in relation to reports or matters broadcast by means of wireless telegraphy as part of any programme or service provided by means of a broadcasting station within the United Kingdom, and in relation to any broadcasting by means of wireless telegraphy of any such report or matter, as they apply in relation to reports and matters published in a newspaper and to publication in a newspaper; and subsection (2) of the said section seven shall have effect, in relation to any such broadcasting, as if for the words "in the newspaper in which" there were substituted the words "in the manner in which".

(3) In this section "broadcasting station" means any station in respect of which a licence granted by the Postmaster General under the enactments relating to wireless telegraphy is in force, being a licence which (by whatever form of words) authorises the use of the station for the purpose of providing broadcasting services for general reception.

Limitation on privilege at elections

10. A defamatory statement published by or on behalf of a candidate in any election to a local government authority or to Parliament shall not be deemed to be published on a privileged occasion on the ground that it is material to a question in issue in the election, whether or not the person by whom it is published is qualified to vote at the election.

Agreements for indemnity

11. An agreement for indemnifying any person against civil liability for libel in respect of the publication of any matter shall not be unlawful unless at the time of the publication that person knows that the matter is defamatory, and does not reasonably believe there is a good defence to any action brought upon it.

Evidence of other damages recovered by plaintiff

12. In any action for libel or slander the defendant may give evidence in mitigation of damages that the plaintiff has recovered damages, or has brought actions for damages, for libel or slander in respect of the publication of words to the same effect as the words on which the action is founded, or has received or agreed to receive compensation in respect of any such publication.

Consolidation of actions for slander, &c.

13. Section five of the Law of Libel Amendment Act, 1888 (which provides for the consolidation, on the application of the defendants, of two or more actions for libel by the same plaintiff) shall apply to actions for slander and to actions for slander of title, slander of goods or other malicious falsehood as it applies to actions for libel; and references in that section to the same, or substantially the same, libel shall be construed accordingly.

Application of Act to Scotland

14. This Act shall apply to Scotland subject to the following modifications, that is to say:—

(*a*) sections one, two, eight and thirteen shall be omitted;
(*b*) for section three there shall be substituted the following section—

"Actions for verbal injury.

3. In any action for verbal injury it shall not be necessary for the pursuer to aver or prove special damage if the words on which the action is founded are calculated to cause pecuniary damage to the pursuer.";

(*c*) subsection (2) of section four shall have effect as if at the end thereof there were added the words "Nothing in this subsection shall be held to entitle a defender to lead evidence of any fact specified in the declaration unless notice of his intention so to do has been given in the defences."; and

(*d*) for any reference to libel, or to libel or slander, there shall be substituted a reference to defamation; the expression "plaintiff" means pursuer; the expression "defendant" means defender; for any reference to an affidavit made by any person there shall be substituted a reference to a written declaration signed by that person; for any reference to the High Court there shall be substituted a reference to the Court of Session or, if an action of defamation is depending in the sheriff court in respect of the publication in question, the sheriff; the expression "costs" means expenses; and for any reference to a defence of justification there shall be substituted a reference to a defence of *veritas*.

Legislative powers of Parliament of Northern Ireland

15. No limitation on the powers of the Parliament of Northern Ireland imposed by the Government of Ireland Act, 1920, shall preclude that Parliament from making laws for purposes similar to the purposes of this Act.

Interpretation

16.—(1) Any reference in this Act to words shall be construed as including a reference to pictures, visual images, gestures and other methods of signifying meaning.

(2) The provisions of Part III of the Schedule to this Act shall have effect for the purposes of the interpretation of that Schedule.

(3) In this Act "broadcasting by means of wireless telegraphy" means publication for general reception by means of wireless telegraphy within the meaning of the Wireless Telegraphy Act, 1949, and "broadcast by means of wireless telegraphy" shall be construed accordingly.

(4) Where words broadcast by means of wireless telegraphy are simultaneously transmitted by telegraph as defined by the Telegraph Act, 1863, in accordance with a licence granted by the Postmaster General the provisions of this Act shall apply as if the transmission were broadcasting by means of wireless telegraphy.

Proceedings affected and saving

17.—(1) This Act applies for the purposes of any proceedings begun after the commencement of this Act, whenever the cause of action arose, but does not affect any proceedings begun before the commencement of this Act.

(2) Nothing in this Act affects the law relating to criminal libel.

Short title, commencement, extent and repeals

18.—(1) This Act may be cited as the Defamation Act, 1952, and shall come into operation one month after the passing of this Act.

(2) This Act (except section fifteen) shall not extend to Northern Ireland.

(3) Sections four and six of the Law of Libel Amendment Act, 1888, are hereby repealed.

SCHEDULE

Sections 7, 16

NEWSPAPER STATEMENTS HAVING QUALIFIED PRIVILEGE

PART I

Statements Privileged without Explanation or Contradiction

1. A fair and accurate report of any proceedings in public of the legislature of any part of Her Majesty's dominions outside Great Britain.

2. A fair and accurate report of any proceedings in public of an international organisation of which the United Kingdom or Her Majesty's Government in the United Kingdom is a member, or of any international conference to which that government sends a representative.

3. A fair and accurate report of any proceedings in public of an international court.

4. A fair and accurate report of any proceedings before a court exercising jurisdiction throughout any part of Her Majesty's dominions outside the United Kingdom, or of any proceedings before a court-martial held outside the United Kingdom under the Naval Discipline Act, the Army Act or the Air Force Act.

5. A fair and accurate report of any proceedings in public of a body or person appointed to hold a public inquiry by the government or legislature of any part of Her Majesty's dominions outside the United Kingdom.

6. A fair and accurate copy of or extract from any register kept in pursuance of any Act of Parliament which is open to inspection by the public, or of any other document which is required by the law of any part of the United Kingdom to be open to inspection by the public.

7. A notice or advertisement published by or on the authority of any court within the United Kingdom or any judge or officer of such a court.

PART II

Statements Privileged Subject to Explanation or Contradiction

8. A fair and accurate report of the findings or decision of any of the following associations, or of any committee or governing body thereof, that is to say—

(*a*) an association formed in the United Kingdom for the purpose of promoting or encouraging the exercise of or interest in any art, science, religion or learning, and empowered by its constitution to exercise control over or adjudicate upon matters of interest or concern to the association, or the actions or conduct of any persons subject to such control or adjudication;

(*b*) an association formed in the United Kingdom for the purpose of promoting or safeguarding the interests of any trade, business, industry or profession, or of the persons carrying on or engaged in any trade, business, industry or profession, and empowered by its constitution to exercise control over or adjudicate upon matters connected with the trade, business, industry or profession, or the actions or conduct of those persons;

(*c*) an association formed in the United Kingdom for the purpose of promoting or safeguarding the interests of any game, sport or pastime to the playing or exercise of which members of the public are invited or admitted, and empowered by its constitution to exercise control over or adjudicate upon persons connected with or taking part in the game, sport or pastime.

being a finding or decision relating to a person who is a member of or is subject by virtue of any contract to the control of the association.

9. A fair and accurate report of the proceedings at any public meeting held in the United Kingdom, that is to say, a meeting bona

fide and lawfully held for a lawful purpose and for the furtherance or discussion of any matter of public concern, whether the admission to the meeting is general or restricted.

10. A fair and accurate report of the proceedings at any meeting or sitting in any part of the United Kingdom of—

(*a*) any local authority or committee of a local authority or local authorities;

(*b*) any justice or justices of the peace acting otherwise than as a court exercising judicial authority;

(*c*) any commission, tribunal, committee or person appointed for the purposes of any inquiry by Act of Parliament, by Her Majesty or by a Minister of the Crown;

(*d*) any person appointed by a local authority to hold a local inquiry in pursuance of any Act of Parliament;

(*e*) any other tribunal, board, committee or body constituted by or under, and exercising functions under, an Act of Parliament,

not being a meeting or sitting admission to which is denied to representatives of newspapers and other members of the public.

11. A fair and accurate report of the proceedings at a general meeting of any company or association constituted, registered or certified by or under any Act of Parliament or incorporated by Royal Charter, not being a private company within the meaning of the Companies Act, 1948.

12. A copy or fair and accurate report or summary of any notice or other matter issued for the information of the public by or on behalf of any government department, officer of state, local authority or chief officer of police.

PART III

Interpretation

13. In this Schedule the following expressions have the meanings hereby respectively assigned to them, that is to say:—

"Act of Parliament" includes an Act of the Parliament of Northern Ireland, and the reference to the Companies Act, 1948, includes a reference to any corresponding enactment of the Parliament of Northern Ireland;

"government department" includes a department of the Government of Northern Ireland;

"international court" means the International Court of Justice and any other judicial or arbitral tribunal deciding matters in dispute between States;

"legislature", in relation to any territory comprised in Her Majesty's dominions which is subject to a central and a local legislature, means either of those legislatures;

"local authority" means any authority or body to which the Local Authorities (Admission of the Press to Meetings) Act, 1908, or the Local Government (Ireland) Act, 1902, as amended by any enactment of the Parliament of Northern Ireland, applies;

"part of Her Majesty's dominions" means the whole of any territory within those dominions which is subject to a separate legislature.

14. In relation to the following countries and territories, that is to say, India, the Republic of Ireland, any protectorate, protected state or trust territory within the meaning of the British Nationality Act, 1948, any territory administered under the authority of a country mentioned in subsection (3) of section one of that Act, the Sudan and the New Hebrides, the provisions of this Schedule shall have effect as they have effect in relation to Her Majesty's dominions, and references therein to Her Majesty's dominions shall be construed accordingly.

TABLE OF STATUTES REFERRED TO IN THIS ACT

Short Title	Session and Chapter
Parliamentary Papers Act, 1840	3 & 4 Vict. c. 9.
Telegraph Act, 1863	26 & 27 Vict. c. 112
Law of Libel Amendment Act, 1888	51 & 52 Vict. c. 64.
Local Government (Ireland) Act, 1902	2 Edw. 7, c. 38.
Local Authorities (Admission of the Press to Meetings) Act, 1908	8 Edw. 7, c. 43.
Government of Ireland Act, 1920	10 & 11 Geo. 5, c. 67.
Companies Act, 1948	11 & 12 Geo. 6, c. 38.
British Nationality Act, 1948	11 & 12 Geo. 6, c. 56.
Wireless Telegraphy Act, 1949	12, 13 & 14 Geo. 6, c. 54.

Bibliography

Current Law, Sweet & Maxwell, Stevens & Sons, 1963, 11 New Fetter Lane, London, E.C. 4.

Modern Advertising Law, by PETER LANGDON-DAVIES, Business Publications Limited, 1963, 180 Fleet Street, London, E.C. 4.

Hatred, Ridicule or Contempt, a book of libel cases by JOSEPH DEAN, Constable, 1953, 10–12 Orange Street, London, W.C. 2.

General Principles of the Law of Torts, by PHILLIP S. JAMES, Butterworths, 1964, 88 Kingsway, London, W.C. 2.

Discovering the Law, by JAMES DERRIMAN, University of London Press, 1962, Warwick Square, London, E.C. 4.

Halsbury's Laws of England, 3rd edn., Simonds edition, in particular vol. 24, *Libel and Slander*, by the HON. SIR GERALD OSBORNE SLADE, one of the Justices of Her Majesty's High Court of Justice, and RICHARD O'SULLIVAN, Esq., Q.C., a Bencher of the Middle Temple, one of Her Majesty's Counsel, Recorder of Derby, Butterworths, 1958, 88 Kingsway, London, W.C. 2.

Gatley on Libel and Slander, 6th edn., by ROBERT L. MCEWEN, Esq., M.A., of the Inner Temple, Barrister at Law and P. S. C. LEWIS, Esq., M.A., of Lincolns Inn, Barrister at Law, Sweet & Maxwell, 1960, 11 New Fetter Lane, London, E.C. 4.

U.K. Press Gazette, Bouverie Publishing Co. Ltd., 2–3 Salisbury Court, Fleet Street, London, E.C. 3 (weekly for Journalists).

The English and Empire Digest, replacement volume No. 32, *Libel and Slander*, by C. A. COLLINGWOOD, Esq., M.A., LL.B., CECIL B. RAMAGE, Esq., B.A., and C. C. CARUS-WILSON, Esq., M.C., B.A., Barristers-at-Law, Butterworths, 1964, 88 Kingsway, London, W.C. 2.

Essential Law for Journalists, 2nd edn., edited by L. C. J. MCNAE, former Head of the Press Association's Special Reporting Service, Staples Press, 1964, 9 Grape Street, London, W.C. 2.

The Kemsley Manual of Journalism, Cassell & Co., 1950, London.

Index

113

57802

KD
L5

LLOYD, HERBERT
THE LEGAL LIMITS OF JOURNALISM.

DATE DUE

APR 27 2010

GAYLORD

PRINTED IN U.S.A.